GLORY DAYS

Buses on the Isle of Wight

Glyn Kraemer-Johnson
and John Bishop

Ian Allan
PUBLISHING

First published 2006

ISBN (10) 0 7110 3114 2
ISBN (13) 978 0 7110 3114 2

Published by Ian Allan Publishing

an imprint of Ian Allan Publishing Ltd, Hersham, Surrey KT12 4RG

Printed in England by Ian Allan Printing Ltd, Hersham, Surrey KT12 4RG

Code: 0611/B

Visit the Ian Allan Publishing website at www.ianallanpublishing.com

Front cover: The popularity of open-top buses in the 1950s and '60s greatly extended the lives of some vehicles. Seen at Ryde in the mid-1960s, ECW-bodied Bristol K5G 906 (FHT 112) was new to Bristol Tramways in 1938 and converted to open-top in the mid-1950s by Brighton, Hove & District, finally being sold to Southern Vectis in 1962. Note the Bristol K type on route 6 and the Lyons Cakes BMC lorry with 'threepenny bit' cab. *Howard Butler*

Back cover: Travelling from Shanklin to Ventnor one passes the turning for Luccombe Chine, near to where this view was recorded *c*1970. With Sandown Bay as a backdrop 1954-built Bristol LD6G 508 (KDL 404) heads in the direction of Ventnor. *Dave Brown*

Title page: A classic early-1960s scene at Sandown Bay. Its five-cylinder Gardner engine hard at work, Bristol LL5G/ECW 842 (HDL 285) climbs from the Esplanade at Shanklin *en route* for the small airport at Sandown. The service operated on summer Saturdays, linking the airport with various hotels in the area. New in 1952, the bus would be withdrawn in 1966. *Howard Butler*

CONTENTS

Narrative by Glyn Kraemer-Johnson
Photographs selected and captioned by John Bishop

Many visitors to the Isle of Wight in the 1950s, '60s and '70s would arrive at Ryde on the ferry from Portsmouth, disembarking at the far end of the pier; from there they would either catch the pier tram or train — or (if it were a fine day) walk. At the landward end of the pier, at Ryde Esplanade, they would catch sight of their first Southern Vectis or Seaview Services bus. This commercial view from the early 1970s features a fine selection of the former, including a Bristol LD, an FLF, two LHs and a Leyland National, as well as prewar ex-London Underground trains plying to and fro along the pier. *Salmon Postcards / Glyn Kraemer-Johnson collection*

INTRODUCTION

When you lose a loved one it's not unusual to try to find what amounts to a replica, someone whose looks, personality and characteristics are as close as possible to those of the departed. Sometimes it works; more often than not it doesn't. I was lucky, but then the loved one I lost was the Brighton, Hove & District Omnibus Co Ltd. It was a love that had lasted more than twenty years. I knew every bus, every advert, every squealing brake, every grinding gearbox . . . and suddenly it was gone. 'SOUTHDOWN-BH&D' began to appear as a fleetname, my beloved KSWs were replaced by 'Queen Mary' Leyland PD3s, and Lodekkas emerged from the paintshop in Southdown green and cream — a lovely livery (on a Leyland), but to me it never looked right on a Lodekka. Finally the whole identity was swallowed up by Southdown, disappearing under a sea of leaf green.

That was when I turned to Southern Vectis, on the Isle of Wight. It was a company of similar size, formerly part of the Tilling Group, it operated Bristol/ECW products and, like BH&D, it had a lot of individuality. In addition, it operated single-deckers and coaches, and its vehicles ran through some of the most beautiful scenery in the South of England. And, of course, the island's open-top services had been inaugurated using ex-BH&D AEC Regents, subsequently replaced by Bristol K5Gs, many of which emanated from the same source.

I had first visited the Isle of Wight in the mid-'Sixties, a visit that engendered a love affair with the island which has lasted to this day. I love its coastline, its picturesque villages and, most of all, I love to get away from the resorts and tourist attractions and enjoy its lesser-known locations, which, fortunately, the majority of holidaymakers are too lazy to discover. I loved the crossing from Portsmouth when it could be made on a 'proper' boat — *Southsea* or *Brading* — and one could stand on deck and watch the silhouette of All Saints' Church, Ryde, growing closer; then the journey down the pier on an antique steam train or, later, an equally antique ex-London tube train, at the end of which, amongst the green-and-cream Bristols, would invariably be waiting one of the two red-and-green all-Leyland PD2s of Seaview Services, then the island's only independent stage-carriage operator.

In those days few people bothered to take their cars to the island. Ferries were so expensive and the bus services so good that it was hardly worthwhile. A Rover ticket was sufficient to ensure you could reach almost any part of the island.

I can still remember my first-ever ride on a Southern Vectis bus, at the rear of the top deck on a fully laden lowbridge Bristol KSW5G. On the journey from Shanklin to Yarmouth my head came into contact with the roof on more than one occasion, and the combination of the island roads and the Gardner 5LW managed to affect parts that other buses could not reach. I was to enjoy an equally memorable journey some years later, when the 1939 K5G (CDL 899) took part in the London–Brighton Historic Commercial Vehicle run, and I managed to secure a ride on the top deck from Brighton to Portsmouth; the imprint of the slatted wooden seats remained on my posterior for several days afterwards. Wonderful stuff!

There are so many memories of the island and its buses, and we hope we have captured some of them within the pages of this book. It is not intended to be a concise history of the island's operators, nor a technical review of their vehicles and services. What we have tried to produce is a light-hearted and non-technical look at the stage-carriage operators and their vehicles in a location that has a special place in our hearts. Not unnaturally the book deals mainly with Southern Vectis, as the island's major bus company, but other stage-carriage operators are included. However, the title of the book is *Glory Days: Buses on the Isle of Wight*, so there are only passing references to the island's many coach operators.

Other books in this series by the same authors have taken the 'Glory Days' as being the years from 1929, when the bus as we know it today was first introduced in the form of the Leyland Titan and AEC Regent, through to 1969 and the formation of the National Bus Company, when boundaries were changed and familiar names and liveries disappeared. With this volume 1929 is an even more appropriate starting point, being the year in which the Southern Vectis Omnibus Co was formed. Fixing an 'end date' was not so simple, for its location protected Southern Vectis from the mergers and changes of area that took place elsewhere,

and the NBC green and white was not *that* different from the original Tilling green and cream. Even under privatisation the company has remained in its management's ownership until recently (mid-2005). Thus, whilst we have retained the period 1929-1969 as being the true 'Glory Days' we have, in this instance, taken the story a little further.

Whilst 1929 is the obvious starting date, it is probably appropriate at this point to set the scene by outlining the events that led to the formation of Southern Vectis.

Strangely, as far as bus operation is concerned there appear to have been links between the Isle of Wight and Brighton since the earliest days. The first motor bus to commence operation on the island did so in April 1905, when the Isle of Wight Express Motor Syndicate introduced a circular service from Ryde via Sandown, Shanklin and Newport. The vehicles used were Milnes-Daimlers with open-top double-deck bodywork, but in those days the condition of the island's roads left much to be desired, and the double-deckers were found to be unsuitable. Within six months they had been replaced by single-deckers, also of Milnes-Daimler manufacture. Additional routes were introduced but proved unprofitable, and after only two years the company found itself in receivership, the appointed Receiver being none other than A. Douglas Mackenzie, who later went on to help found Brighton-based Southdown Motor Services Ltd.

There was little further development in the island's road transport until the early 'Twenties, when the lack of public transport attracted the attention of one Frank Dodson, a Londoner whose family owned a successful coachbuilding business in Willesden. Interestingly Dodson built many bodies for Thomas Tilling Ltd, which used them on both its London and Brighton operations, the latter being the forerunner of Brighton, Hove & District. Frank Dodson began operating bus services on the island in 1921 using Daimlers with, not unnaturally, Dodson bodies, the vehicles being housed in an aerodrome at Somerton, on the outskirts of Cowes. Further services were introduced, connecting Newport with Cowes, Ryde, Sandown, Shanklin and Carisbrooke, as well as

UNION ST., RYDE.

Shanklin with Sandown and with Ryde. In 1922 Frank Dodson was joined by his brother, Leonard, and the business became known as 'Dodson Bros, trading as the Vectis Bus Service'. A blue, red and white livery was used.

In October 1927 a devastating fire swept through the depot at Somerton, destroying no fewer than 13 buses. Services were maintained with the help of vehicles loaned by the island's other operators and by the London General Omnibus Co. In spite of this setback and fierce competition Vectis continued to expand both westward to Yarmouth and Alum Bay and southward to Ventnor, establishing a network of services that remained virtually unchanged until the summer of 1929, when the Southern Vectis Omnibus Company Ltd was formed and when our story 'proper' begins.

Acknowledgements
The authors would like to thank all those who have contributed photographs and other items for inclusion in this book. In particular, thanks go to Martin Rickett, for supplying the tickets that have been reproduced, and to the Isle of Wight Bus & Coach Museum, for allowing us to photograph its memorabilia. Thanks are due also to Grahame and Keith Bowler, Richard Newman and Don Vincent, for the help and advice they have given us 'Overners'!

Glyn Kraemer-Johnson
Hailsham, East Sussex
July 2006

This 1921 photograph depicts three Vectis Bus Co Daimler Y-type buses (DL 2446-8) that commenced services, plus a short-lived Thornycroft (DL 2491); all were bodied by Dodson, which firm had been established by the same family that set up the Isle of Wight business. The garage at Somerton Airport would be comparatively short-lived, being replaced by one at Newport. Daimler DL 2446, meanwhile, would be destroyed in a fire at the airport in 1927. *Pamlin Prints / R. H. Davies collection*

The drivers and conductors seemed to take great delight in having their photographs taken, and the young conductor here looks smart in his uniform and gaiters, which are highly polished — a habit no doubt instilled as a result of National Service in the Great War. Recorded as a Daimler Y with Dodson body, No 6 (DL 2937) of 1922 clearly has an AEC radiator, demonstrating the close ties between the two companies in their early years. *R. H. Davies / Glyn Kraemer-Johnson collection*

The Vectis Bus Co continued its allegiance to Daimler with this Dodson-bodied CK, No 28 (DL 5175). Delivered in 1927, it clearly shows the refinements over the earlier Daimler Y model; note in particular the full-drop windows, of which full use is being made on what looks to have been a hot summer's day in the late 1920s. *R. H. Davies / Glyn Kraemer-Johnson collection*

5

1. SINGLE-DECKS RULE, OK!

The year 1923 had seen the establishment of the 'Big Four' railway companies, the Southern, Great Western (GWR), London, Midland & Scottish (LMS) and London & North Eastern (LNER). As far as the Isle of Wight was concerned this meant that the island's three railways — the Isle of Wight Railway, the Isle of Wight Central and the Freshwater, Newport & Yarmouth — became part of the Southern Railway. More pertinent to our story is the fact that in 1928 an Act was passed empowering the railway companies to provide bus services. However, rather than engaging in wasteful competition the railway companies decided on a strategy of buying into or, in some cases, purchasing outright established bus operators. Most notable amongst the former was probably the National Omnibus Co, which had operations stretching from East Anglia to Cornwall. Following investment by the Southern Railway, the GWR and the LNER this became three companies —

Southern National, Western National and Eastern National. When a similar arrangement was mooted for the Isle of Wight the Dodson brothers agreed to the Southern Railway's taking a 50% share in their Vectis Bus Co. Consequently a new company came into being in March 1929 with its head office at Waterloo station and known as the Southern Vectis Omnibus Co Ltd.

Following a strike by SVOC staff, the Dodson brothers decided to retire in 1932, selling their 50% share of the company to the Tilling & British Automobile Traction group, something which was to have considerable influence on Southern Vectis policy in later years.

The company's head office was re-established at St James's Square, Newport, instead of Waterloo, and Mr Walter Budd was brought in as General Manager. Budd had previously been manager of Southdown Motor Services'

In 1926 AEC and Daimler formed a partnership known as Associated Daimler. However, this alliance was short-lived, and in 1928 the two companies went their separate ways. One of the first models to be sold by the newly independent AEC was the Reliance chassis, and the 'new' Southern Vectis company was an eager customer, taking an initial batch of 13 (49-61) in 1930 and a further three (67-9) in 1931, all with dual-doorway Dodson bodywork; pictured is 60 (DL 7065). The radiator design would shortly give way to the now familiar Regent/ Regal style, which was to last into the postwar era.
The Omnibus Society

Portsmouth division and brought with him not only a period of co-operation with Southdown but also that company's elegant livery of apple green and cream with dark-green lining, which replaced the old Vectis blue and red.

At the time of SVOC's formation competition was fierce and services were chaotic, with any number of operators endeavouring to 'cream off' passengers from the more profitable routes, leaving other areas virtually unserved. The 1930 Road Traffic Act brought order out of chaos, requiring operators to apply to the newly appointed Traffic Commissioners for licences to operate both vehicles and services.

Sensing that the Act would make life more difficult for them, a number of the smaller operators decided to sell out to Southern Vectis before its introduction. These included Casey of Ryde, Bullock of Havenstreet (t/a Surprise Bus Services), Creeth of Nettlestone (t/a Premier Motors) and the bus services of the Isle of Wight Tourist Co. Most of the services operated were based on Ryde and Newport and brought with them a motley collection of single-deck buses and charabancs, mainly of AEC, Dennis and Guy manufacture. Most were numbered into the Southern Vectis fleet, only a handful not being operated. The Creeth operation included a garage at Nettlestone. Both Creeth and the IoW

Tourist Co had been part of a trio of operators involved in a stage-carriage service between Ryde and Seaview, but their acquisition by SVOC left the third participant, R. Newell, as the sole operator of the service.

The fleet inherited from the Vectis Bus Co had consisted of some 36 vehicles, mainly of Daimler and ADC (Associated Daimler) manufacture, together with some Guys and Chevrolets for good measure. Thus by 1930 the fleet was far from standardised.

The first new vehicles to be acquired by Southern Vectis arrived in early 1929 in the shape of six AEC 426s with 32-seat Dodson bodywork, unusual in being of dual-door layout. They were registered DL 6155-60 and given fleet numbers 38-43, though not in order. In 1930 the company took delivery of 13 AEC Reliances (DL 6829-38, 7064-6) with similar dual-door bodywork, again by Dodson, a further three (DL 7385-7) arriving the following year.

This was the time of the Dodson brothers' retirement and the acquisition of their shares by the Tilling-BAT group, which immediately stamped its own vehicle policy on the company. A solitary AEC Regal (DL 7811) arrived in 1932, the last of its kind apart from a few coaches bought later in the decade.

In 1929 AEC introduced its Regal chassis, which shared many components with the manufacturer's successful Regent double-decker, and in 1931 Southern Vectis took delivery of 70 (DL 7811) with rear-entrance Dodson bodywork, shown here in pristine condition, possibly following exhibition at that year's Commercial Motor Show. Note the pump for the Autovac system for the fuel on the front nearside; also the large sidelight and the 'lollipop' mounted on the wing, to help the driver judge the extremity of the bodywork.
R. H. Davies / Pamlin Prints

In 1932/3 Southern Vectis took delivery of six Tilling-Stevens saloons. No doubt the choice was influenced by the then new General Manager, Walter Budd, who had previously served with Southdown Motor Services, which already had a substantial fleet of similar machines. The first two (Nos 71/2) were bodied by Dodson and very similar in appearance to the AEC Regal delivered in 1931, but the other four were bodied to a similar style by Brush, another new supplier for Southern Vectis; No 104 (DL 8437) is pictured in as-delivered condition. This fine-looking vehicle would last only eight years, being withdrawn in 1941. *R. H. Davies*

By the time 506 (DL 9006) was delivered in 1934 Southern Vectis was part of the Tilling/BAT combine. A Dennis Lancet — another new chassis type for the company — with Eastern Counties bodywork, it is seen at Ryde. In 1944 this vehicle, along with others of its type, would be rebodied by Eastern Coach Works, in which form it was to survive into the early 1950s. *The Omnibus Society*

Exhibited at the 1931 Commercial Motor Show, it carried the usual 32-seat Dodson body but with a single rear door. Similar bodywork, but of 35-seat capacity, was carried by the other two buses delivered new that year, but these were mounted on the then popular Tilling-Stevens B49A chassis. Shortly after their arrival the fleet was renumbered, a separate number series being allocated to each vehicle type, the two TSMs starting a new series as 100/1 (DL 7991/2).

Whether the change of chassis manufacturer was influenced by the Tilling involvement in the company or whether it was due to Mr Budd's experience of the type with Southdown (for which company it was the standard single-deck chassis) is not recorded, but a further four (DL 8435-8) arrived in 1933. However, these had 35-seat bodywork by Brush and signified the end of the company's association with Dodson bodywork.

The final ties with the Dodson brothers were severed in 1934 when Southern Vectis moved out of the garage at Somerton and into new purpose-built premises at Nelson Road, Newport — buildings which serve as the company's head office and works to this day.

The mid-'Thirties might be called 'the Dennis years' so far as vehicle policy was concerned. In the autumn of 1933 a Dennis Lancet demonstrator had been on loan for evaluation purposes, and, presumably as a result of this, 10 Dennis Lancets (DL 9000-9) were delivered in the early summer of 1934. These had 36-seat rear-entrance bodywork by Eastern Counties (later to become Eastern Coach Works) and featured full-length roof luggage racks, which gave them a somewhat bulbous appearance. They marked the beginning of a relationship with the coachbuilder that was to endure until closure of the Eastern Coach Works factory in 1987.

In the mid-'Thirties the island's roads were still considered unsuitable for double-deckers, and trunk routes were worked by the larger saloons with around 35 seats, duplicates being operated as required. However, there was still a need for smaller vehicles, and to meet this six 20-seat Dennis Aces were delivered with registration numbers following on from the Lancets (DL 9010-5). Bodied by Thomas Harrington of Hove, they were allocated fleet numbers 400-5. The Ace was a 'normal control' chassis, *i.e.* with the driver sitting behind the engine rather than beside it. The front wheels were set back being almost underneath the driver's cab and the resultant protruding bonnet earned these little vehicles the nickname of 'flying pig'. Elegant they may not have been, but they were useful little workhorses and were quite long-lived. In fact one (DL 9013) was converted into a lorry and remained in the company's service until the end of 1959, finally being scrapped in 1962.

More Lancets (DL 9700-12) arrived in 1935, this time with 36-seat bodywork by Harrington. They were outwardly very similar to the Eastern Counties version, the front in particular being very severe for the Hove coachbuilder.

Like most major companies at the time Southern Vectis continued to expand by the acquisition of smaller operators. King of Carisbrooke and Morris of Ventnor — both operators of town services, the former in Newport, the latter in Ventnor — had been acquired in 1934, but a more noteworthy purchase, in 1935, was Brown's Bus Service, also of Carisbrooke. This concern incorporated the West Wight Bus Service and brought with it a Newport–Yarmouth–Freshwater service as well as local services in West Wight and, importantly, a depot at Freshwater, giving SVOC a firm footing in this part of the island. Involved in the takeover was a motley collection of vehicles, including such makes as Star, Chevrolet and Dodge, together with a number of Dennises. Few stayed with Southern Vectis for long, and all but one had gone by the outbreak of World War 2. (The survivor was DL 7090, a Dennis Lancet with locally-built Margham bodywork new in 1932, which fitted quite comfortably into the SVOC fleet and lasted until 1941, when it passed to the War Department.)

Also in 1934 Southern Vectis took into stock six 20-seat Harrington-bodied Dennis Aces. Our view depicts the first, 400 (DL 9010), in Newport on a far-from-ideal day for the long haul to Yarmouth, in the west of the island. Despite its small size it still has provision for luggage at the rear, on the roof. *The Omnibus Society*

The Harrington-bodied Dennis Aces lasted well into the postwar period, as demonstrated by this view of 405 (DL 9015) in St James's Square, Newport; behind an example of the equally useful Bedford OB, 210 (EDL 638) can just be seen. Fortunately 405 would survive to be rescued for preservation and can today be found at the Isle of Wight Bus & Coach Museum, where it serves as a fitting reminder of prewar rural transport. *Eric Surfleet*

Although Southern Vectis was now firmly under Tilling/BAT control General Manager Walter Budd still had some sway in terms of vehicle policy, specifying Harrington bodywork (built deep in the heart of Southdown territory) for a batch of 13 Dennis Lancets delivered in 1935. Fortunately some crews loved to be photographed, hence this view of a sparkling 517 (DL 9707) at Ryde when virtually new. This vehicle was to serve the company for a creditable 15 years, retaining its original body throughout. *The Omnibus Society*

Two more Lancets arrived in 1936 showing a
return to Eastern Counties bodywork. Numbered
consecutively as 524/5 (ADL 506/7), they were,
however, quite different. No 524 was a Dennis
Lancet I and had a 35-seat rear-entrance body
basically similar to the 1934 Lancets, although
the luggage rack was confined to the rear of the
roof and the bodywork showed some traces of
Harrington influence. Delivered at the same
time, 525 was built on an early Lancet II chassis
and consequently had a larger 6.7-litre
petrol engine, a taller, slimmer radiator and
lacked the front bumper of the Lancet I; it had 32
high-backed seats and was classified as a dual-
purpose vehicle. When new both buses carried
the attractive livery of apple green lower panels
with dark green roof and window surrounds
separated by a cream waistband and with a cream 'advert panel'
at roof level, but by 1949 No 525 had received coach livery of
cream with green waistband and mudguards.

Also delivered in 1936 were a further two Harrington-bodied
Dennis Aces, 406/7 (ADL 508/9). Originally fitted with four-
cylinder Dennis petrol engines, they later had these replaced by
six-cylinder Bedford diesel units.

Walkden's of Sandown operated services on the trunk
Ryde–Brading–Shanklin corridor as well as between Sandown
and Bembridge. Its acquisition in 1936 brought into the Southern
Vectis fleet some interesting vehicles, including three Morris
Commercials — two Viceroys and a Director — all of which had
bodywork by the Hampshire firm of Strachans. The Viceroys
remained in the fleet until 1938, the Director lasting a year longer.

Much longer-lived were two
Leyland Cubs with dual-purpose
bodywork, also by Strachans;
numbered 50/1 (DL 9086, 9680),
they would remain with Southern
Vectis until 1951. Another Morris,
a Dictator with Thurgood body,
came into SVOC ownership in 1937
together with a miscellany of
vehicles acquired with the business
of Pioneer (Coffen) of Ryde.
The Morris was sold after two years,
but the Pioneer fleet also included
DL 9043, a Dennis Ace with
Harrington 20-seat body, which
fitted in nicely with the vehicles of
this type already owned by Southern
Vectis; requisitioned by the War
Department in 1941, it would return
to the island in 1945, ironically not

to Southern Vectis but to Nash of Ventnor, with which operator it was to give a further 10 years' service.

The year 1937 was in fact quite a significant one for Southern Vectis. Until that time the company had been happy to leave coaching work to the smaller operators. However, in July 1937 it acquired the business of Eames of Shanklin, which was solely a coach operator, although it did operate an express service from Ryde to the Brighstone Holiday Camp. The Eames fleet was mainly of Dennis manufacture but also included two AEC Regals with Harrington coachwork (BDL 313/4) delivered around the time of the takeover.

The second noteworthy event of 1937 was the arrival of the first vehicles of Bristol manufacture. The purchase of Bristol/ECW products was being actively encouraged by the Tilling & BAT group, of which Southern Vectis was part, and Bristol was to become the major supplier of chassis until the company ceased production in the early 'Eighties. The first two Bristol single-deckers (BDL 102/3) were of type JO5G, the classification signifying a **J**-type chassis with **O**il (diesel) **5**-cylinder **G**ardner engine, the latter being the 5LW which was also to become the company's standard for many years. The pair had 35-seat rear-entrance bodywork built by Eastern Coach Works (ECW), successor to Eastern Counties, and started a new number series as 800/1.

By 1938 Bristol had introduced new models, these being the K-type double-deck and L-type single-deck chassis. The 1938 single-deck deliveries to SVOC were therefore of type L5G, but their 35-seat bodies were built by J. C. Beadle of Dartford, a coachbuilder that was to become a popular supplier of bus and coach bodies to operators in the South of England. Outwardly the Beadle bodies were virtually identical to those built by ECW

The Leyland Cub was a rival to the Dennis Ace and to the casual eye was similar, with bonnet and normal-control layout, but Leyland also developed a forward-control version (the SKP3), which increased the seating capacity by six. When the Walkden of Sandown business was acquired by Southern Vectis in 1936 two such models, with Strachans bodywork, were taken into stock as 50/1 (DL 9086, 9680), the latter being depicted in this view at Ryde Esplanade. Both would serve the company until 1950. *Southdown Enthusiasts' Club / W. J. Haynes*

Poster advertising stage services between Ryde and Alum Bay. The service numbers were prone to frequent changes. *Isle of Wight Bus & Coach Museum*

In 1937 Southern Vectis, in line with other companies within the Tilling/BAT group, found that standardisation was becoming the key word in the form of Bristol chassis with Eastern Coach Works bodywork. Looking rather past its best at Ryde Esplanade station is the company's first JO5G single-decker, 800 (BDL 102).
The Omnibus Society

apart from a slightly different treatment of the area below the driver's windscreen.

Also delivered in 1938 were two AEC Regals with futuristic-looking streamlined coach bodies by Thomas Harrington, featuring the famous Harrington 'dorsal fin' at the rear. Numbered 17/18 (CDL 94/5), they had been ordered by Eames before its sale to SVOC. Unfortunately both of these fine vehicles were requisitioned by the War Department after only two years' service and were never returned.

The coaching side was further expanded in the summer of 1938 by the purchase of the Isle of Wight Touring Co, which brought with it a selection of coaches of Dennis and Bedford manufacture.

Sixteen more L5Gs arrived in 1939. Fourteen had bus bodies by Harrington of Hove, the remaining two being bodied by

Margham of Newport, creating a rare if not unique combination. They were numbered 809-24 (CDL 600-15). Again there were very few apparent differences between these and the Beadle, Harrington and ECW bodies apart from the treatment of the front dash.

To boost the small-bus fleet two Dennis Falcons were delivered with handsome ECW bodies. The Falcon chassis was designed to take bodywork with a seating capacity of around 30, but the Southern Vectis vehicles seated just 20, with obvious improvement in passenger comfort. They also incorporated sliding roofs and roof-mounted luggage racks, the latter being a feature of most saloons in the fleet. They were numbered in a new series as 200/1 (CDL 900/1). They were in fact the last new vehicles delivered before the outbreak of World War 2, being received in August 1939.

In 1938 Southern Vectis took delivery of its first examples of the Bristol L-type chassis, of which 30, bodied by a variety of builders, would be taken into stock in the years 1938-46; the company would standardise on the L5G model, with five-cylinder Gardner engine. Delivered in 1939, 814 (CDL 605) had a Harrington body, which to the casual observer looked little different from the products of Eastern Coach Works. Alongside in this early-1950s view at Ryde Esplanade is an ex-Cardiff Corporation Leyland Titan TD1, 708 (TF 6821), rebodied by ECW in 1949. *Roy Marshall collection / East Pennine Transport Group*

▲ A close-up study of Harrington-bodied Bristol L5G 819 (CDL 610) of 1938, clearly showing the Autovac fuel system mounted under the front nearside windscreen. Note also the full use of the area above the side windows for advertisements, which feature would continue until the demise of the postwar L types. *Michael Rooum*

▲ Introduced in the late 1930s, the successor to the Dennis Ace was the Falcon; with more æsthetically pleasing radiator. Demonstrating this is Southern Vectis 201 (CDL 901), with 20-seat bodywork by Eastern Coach Works, new in 1939. Note the continuing provision for luggage on the rear portion of the roof. *Roy Marshall collection / East Pennine Transport Group*

Before World War 2 Bedford's offering for the small-coach market was the WTB, the front of which was redesigned in 1938 with a more rounded appearance, as demonstrated here by Southern Vectis 23 (CDL 729). Bodied by Duple and delivered in 1939, it had been ordered by the Isle of Wight Tourist Co prior to that firm's acquisition by Southern Vectis.
Alan B. Cross

The last coaches purchased by Southern Vectis before the outbreak of World War 2 were four AEC Regals (17-20), of which the last two were bought second-hand from Thomas Tilling in 1939; upon acquisition they were rebodied by Harrington, and very handsome they looked too. Requisitioned in 1940 and repurchased in 1943, 19 (GN 1379) had its body refurbished by Saunders following the end of hostilities, enabling it to continue in service until 1953.
The Omnibus Society

Also new, but delivered earlier in the year, as 21-3 (CDL 727-9), were three Bedford WTB coaches with 25-seat Duple bodywork, the first of many coaches of this combination to enter the fleet. Two further coaches added to the fleet in 1939 were a pair of second-hand AEC Regals acquired from Thomas Tilling Ltd of London, which had built their 39-seat bodywork. However, only the chassis were purchased by Southern Vectis, which had them fitted with new 32-seat bodies by Harrington and numbered them 19 and 20 (GN 1379, GO 1409). Again they had the distinctive 'dorsal fin' but were to a more elegant and less flamboyant design than the previous year's deliveries. Again, less than a year after their acquisition, both were requisitioned by the War Department (although 19 would be re-purchased by SVOC in 1943). By this time,

however, coaching activities were beginning to take a back seat, for just two months after these Regals arrived war was declared, and the island's operators had to re-examine their priorities.

2. ENTER THE 'DECKER

Ironically the very first bus service to operate on the Isle of Wight, in 1905, had been worked by Milnes-Daimler double-deckers of the Isle of Wight Express Motor Syndicate. These had been withdrawn and replaced after a mere six months when it was decided that the island's roads were unsuitable for double-deckers, and for the next 30 years bus services remained in the hands of single-deckers.

In 1935 Southern Vectis decided that it wished to operate double-deckers on its trunk routes between Ryde, Newport and East and West Cowes. Application was made to the Traffic Commissioners, but apparently attitudes had not changed, for the application was rejected on the grounds that sections of the routes were still not suitable for double-deck operation. However, SVOC persisted with its application, and eventually the necessary permission was granted. As a result an order was placed for six double-deckers, and these duly arrived on the island during the summer of 1936.

In view of the currently favoured single-decker, it was hardly surprising that the chosen chassis was the Dennis Lance II, with the newly introduced front end and radiator as fitted to Lancet II 525, delivered at the same time. Unlike the single-decker, however, they were powered from new by the Gardner 5LW oil engine.

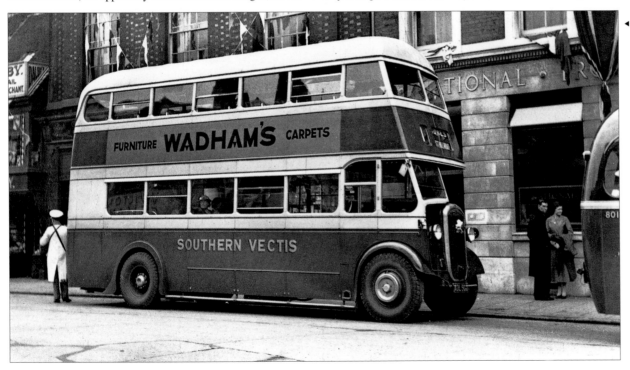

It is hard to believe that the first double-deck deliveries after the short-lived pioneering Milnes-Daimlers of 1905 were six Dennis Lance IIs, delivered to Southern Vectis as late as 1936. Fitted with the then standard Gardner 5LW engine and handsome Eastern Coach Works bodywork, they were finished in Southdown-style apple green and cream with dark-green lining. Pictured c1937 in St James's Square, Newport, on the company's main route to Cowes from Ryde is the first of the batch, 600 (ADL 500); in front can be seen the tail of newly delivered Bristol JO5G 801 (BDL 103).
The Omnibus Society

There is surely a tale to be told in this prewar view on a wet day of Eastern Coach Works-bodied Dennis Lance 605 (ADL 505) standing out from the kerb in St James's Square, Newport, with discussions in progress between the crew and the cyclist. Noteworthy are the advertisements on either side of the destination display for the well-known Isle of Wight store of Dabells, where one could buy 'model hats' for 'popular prices'; also the delightful Standard car from the mainland (betrayed by its Leicester numberplate, BBC 643) and, looming up behind, one of the ex-Colson Bedford WTBs *en route* for Gunville. *The Omnibus Society*

The 56-seat highbridge bodies were built by Eastern Counties and were to that company's standard design, albeit with some modification to the front end to suit the Dennis chassis rather than the Bristol to which they were more normally fitted. Unusual, though not unique, was the fact that they were of five-bay construction (*i.e.* with five main side windows) instead of the six then more customary. Interestingly they were delivered at the time when the Eastern Counties bodybuilding concern became Eastern Coach Works Ltd, and the last two buses of the batch were actually delivered the day after the new company came into being. As a new chassis type they started a new number series as 600-5, registered ADL 500-5 — an early example of SVOC vehicles having closely corresponding fleet and registration numbers, unusual for the time. Livery was again very Southdown-like, being apple green with cream roof and window surrounds, set off with dark green and gold lining-out.

This postwar view of Dennis Lance 603 (ADL 503) in Newport reveals that the Eastern Coach Works body is not shown to best advantage in the later Tilling-green livery, proving the point that an attractive livery can do so much for a fleet. Nevertheless, with the standard Gardner 5LW engine it must have been a dependable machine, serving its owner until 1954 — a period of some 18 years. *Southdown Enthusiasts' Club / W. J. Haynes*

A further two double-deckers joined the fleet in 1937, this time on Bristol GO5G chassis, the double-deck version of the J type. These were in fact the first Bristol vehicles to enter the fleet, the choice of chassis being influenced by the Tilling & BAT; indeed, from this time until closure of the Bristol factory in 1983 all new Southern Vectis double-deck chassis would be of this manufacture. The GO5Gs began another new numbering series as 700/1 and again had closely matching registration numbers (BDL 100/1). They were fitted with 56-seat highbridge bodies by ECW, these being of the more usual six-bay construction; they were, in fact, to a transitional design somewhere between the bodies fitted to the Lances and the final standard prewar ECW double-decker. Their most striking feature was the heavily radiused corners to the top of the front upper-deck windows, commonplace on the products of some Lancashire-based coachbuilders, notably Massey and Northern Counties (the latter incorporating these on early rear-engined double-deckers), but seldom found on ECW products. Whilst 700 led a fairly normal existence on the island, 701 was converted to lowbridge layout by Hants & Dorset in 1951, reducing its seating capacity to 54; this was a rare conversion to be undertaken, due to its complexity and, presumably, its cost.

The lowbridge layout, pioneered by Leyland on the original closed-top Titan in 1927, enabled the height of a double-decker to be reduced by around 12in, allowing it to be used on routes that encountered low bridges and would otherwise have necessitated the use of a single-decker, with an obvious loss of passenger capacity. The reduction in height was achieved by fitting rows of seats for four on the nearside of the top deck and incorporating a sunken gangway on the offside. Whilst this arrangement achieved its objective it was both cumbersome and unpopular; it was difficult for a conductor standing in the sunken gangway to collect fares from those sitting at the opposite end of the seats for four and equally awkward for such passengers to leave a crowded vehicle. Both headroom and visibility were poor for upper-deck passengers, and in those days, when most were smokers, the

Southern Vectis took only two examples of Bristol's first double-deck design, a pair of GO5G models being delivered in 1937 as 700/1 (BDL 100/1). This photograph shows 700 (BDL 100) at Ryde Esplanade station when new; although slightly blurred it shows to good effect the six-bay construction of the prewar Eastern Coach Works body. Surprisingly 701 would be rebuilt to lowbridge configuration in 1951, but 700 was to remain in original guise until withdrawal in 1954. *The Omnibus Society*

Bristol GO5G 700 (BDL 100) in Tilling-green livery in St James's Square, Newport, on a wet day in July 1951, three years before withdrawal. At the time one might have cursed the intrusion of the Southern Vectis employee in summer uniform; now his presence serves as an aid to historians, removing any doubt as to the season. *Alan B. Cross*

atmosphere could get pretty thick! In addition, the sunken gangway protruded into the lower saloon, and many a forgetful or unwary passenger would crack his or her head when leaving an offside seat. (Southern Vectis also specified an overhead luggage rack in the lower saloon that matched the sunken gangway in outline, so even the nearside passengers did not escape this hazard!) However, the lowbridge layout served its purpose and, indeed, was all that was available until the early 'Fifties, when Bristol solved the problem once and for all with its Lodekka. But more of that later.

One more double-decker to join the Southern Vectis fleet before the outbreak of World War 2 was a Bristol K5G fitted with a 56-seat highbridge ECW body. The K-type chassis, double-deck version of the L, had been introduced in 1937 and was to remain in production for 20 years, the usual power unit (as in this case) being the trusty Gardner 5LW. The bodywork was the standard ECW product of the time, similar to that on 700/1 but with more normally shaped windows at the front of the upper deck. 'The Old Girl', as she would become known in later years, arrived on the island in July 1939 and was numbered 702 (CDL 899). Arguably one of the most famous buses ever built, she has long held the record for being the longest-serving bus with its original owner and, at the time of writing, is approaching her 67th birthday. She's even older than your authors (just!) and could easily warrant a book of her own, but with the limited space available here she must be treated much the same as any other member of the fleet.

One more prewar 'decker was to be delivered, but this would not materialise until early 1940, by which time the company's operations were changing radically.

The outbreak of war meant that by 1940 economies were already being made with regard to the delivery of new vehicles. However, some manufacturers had stocks of parts, leading to the release of what were known as 'unfrozen' buses such as Southern Vectis Bristol L5G/ECW 827 (DDL 53), seen postwar at Ryde Esplanade. Note the utility double-decker behind, adding to the scene; also the state of 827's offside front tyre! *W. J. Haynes / Southdown Enthusiasts' Club*

". . . I have to tell you now that no such undertaking has been received and that consequently this country is at war with Germany."

Neville Chamberlain's immortal words coming from almost every wireless set in the country sent the last of the Isle of Wight's summer visitors scurrying for the ferries back to the mainland. With hindsight it could be said that the Government of the day over-reacted; certainly some of its actions were illogical. Two days before war was declared had begun the evacuation from London and the major cities of thousands of children. They were moved to so-called 'safe' locations that included the Kent coast, soon to be virtually in the front line, and the Isle of Wight, itself particularly vulnerable due to its proximity to the ports of Southampton and Portsmouth. The children arrived at the island's railway stations with their gas masks and labels around their necks and Southern Vectis buses ferried them to the towns and villages in which they had been billeted. When it was realised that the Isle of Wight could be under the threat of invasion, particularly after the retreat from Dunkirk in 1940, they were returned home.

Theatres and cinemas were closed, the blackout was introduced and people were advised to stay at home. 'Is your journey really necessary?' became a popular slogan. Along with most coastal towns the Isle of Wight was designated a restricted area, only residents or those on official business being allowed to enter or leave. In the island's case such restrictions were probably easier to enforce, many of the ferries having been requisitioned for use as minesweepers and those that remained operating only a skeleton service. (At least three of the paddle-steamers, PS *Portsdown, Whippingham* and *Sandown*, would play their part in the evacuation from Dunkirk.) These restrictions had a considerable effect on all bus operators, Southern Vectis being no exception. However, the Government soon realised that theatres and especially cinemas not only boosted civilian morale but were also important channels for propaganda, and they were therefore reopened, bringing about an increase in evening traffic for bus operators.

The blackout was probably the biggest hazard, drivers having to manage with masked headlights, no street lamps and with familiar landmarks in darkness. Conductors fared little better:

interior lighting consisted of a few dim blue bulbs, and conductors — or more often 'clippies', as conductresses became known — would fumble with tickets and change whilst holding low-powered torches. Hardest hit of all were the driver/conductors on the one-man-operated 20-seaters. Buses received white-painted edges to mudguards, rear panels and lifeguards to aid visibility and were gradually repainted into dull overall grey (or at least received grey or brown roofs) to minimise recognition from the air.

Petrol and fuel oil were rationed, supplies being reduced by as much as 50%, resulting in severe cuts in services. Late in 1939, in an effort to save fuel, the two Bristol JO5Gs of 1937 were converted to run on producer gas ('produced' by burning coke), the gas units being carried in the rear luggage lockers. Another five vehicles would be similarly converted in 1943/4, but with the gas-producing unit mounted on a trailer towed behind the bus. Vehicles running on producer

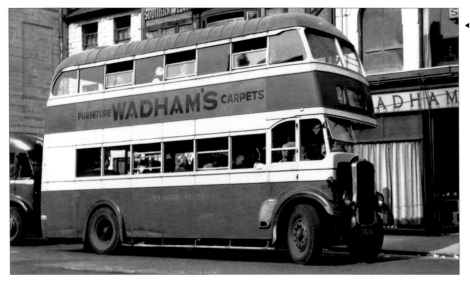

gas proved to be poor performers, particularly on hilly routes, of which Southern Vectis had many, and the conversion programme was not extended further.

Delivered in January 1940 were five new vehicles, all of Bristol/ECW manufacture, construction of which had started before the outbreak of war. Four — L5Gs with 35-seat bodywork and outwardly virtually identical to the Harrington-bodied examples new the previous year — were given fleet numbers 825-8 (DDL 51-4). The fifth vehicle was a Bristol K5G with 56-

seat highbridge body, broadly similar to 702 but with subtle variations. Externally these amounted to little more than a different treatment of the moulding beneath the windscreen. Internally the window frames and trim were of a dark varnished wood (rather than the yellowish wood used on 702), while the light fittings too were different, being mounted on the window pillars and having frosted-glass covers of an almost art-deco design. No 703 (DDL 50) would prove as long-lived as her sister, despite spending only a mere 40 years with Southern Vectis; since

1979 she has been in preservation, beautifully restored, and at the time of writing (July 2006) has recently returned to the island to be exhibited in the Isle of Wight Bus & Coach Museum.

The sudden disappearance of holidaymakers was obviously a severe blow to the island's bus and coach operators, but this was alleviated to some extent by the carriage of workers to/from the factories and shipyards in and around Cowes. The major shipyards were those of Saunders-Roe and J. White; Saunders-Roe concentrated mainly on the construction of seaplanes, whilst White's was engaged in building warships, notably destroyers. Obviously the output of both concerns was of high national importance, and large numbers of workers were employed, most of whom needed to be transported by bus.

The other major source of traffic was, of course, the military. Large numbers of troops had been posted to the island, hotels, guest-houses and other large buildings having been taken over to accommodate them. The Puckpool Holiday Camp had been acquired by the Fleet Air Arm as HMS *Medina*, and this brought extra traffic to Mr Newell's Ryde–Seaview service, on which route it was situated. It was in 1942 that this operator's name, Newell's (Seaview) Ltd, was changed to Seaview Services Ltd.

Following the retreat from Dunkirk the 6th Battalion of the Black Watch was deployed to defend the Isle of Wight. A number of Southern Vectis drivers and their vehicles were actually seconded to the battalion and were permanently on call. They were paid by the Army, slept with their vehicles and grabbed meals whenever they could.

The island's shipyards and military establishments ensured the attention of the Luftwaffe, which on the night of 4/5 May 1942 mounted a concentrated raid on Cowes. Around 160 low-flying German fighter-bombers dropped some 200 tons of bombs and a torrent of incendiaries, followed by high explosives. The Polish destroyer *Blyskawica* was undergoing a refit in White's yard at the time and set up smoke screens to obscure the town before leaving her moorings and dropping anchor outside the harbour; she then used her large-calibre guns to force the enemy aircraft to fly too high for their bombing to be accurate. She fired with such ferocity that more ammunition had to be ferried across from Portsmouth and her guns cooled with water. Nevertheless around 100 people were killed that night and more than 8,000 injured. Along with thousands of buildings White's yard was severely damaged, but without the help of the *Blyskawica* matters would have been far worse. As recently as 2004 an area of Cowes was named *Francki Place* after the Commander of the *Blyskawica*.

Singled out for particular attention from the Luftwaffe was the radar network. Having carried out similar attacks on radar stations at Dover, Rye and Pevensey, the bombers headed for the Chain Home Radar Station at Ventnor, where they caused considerable damage. Most of the buildings were destroyed or damaged, and the station was unable to function, a mobile facility hastily set up at Bembridge being used until repairs had been carried out.

The foregoing were just two of many incidents too numerous to recall here. Miraculously, despite the constant bombing raids, no Southern Vectis vehicles were destroyed, and, although several buses suffered from machine-gun fire, damage was generally light. Indeed, the most damage to the fleet was caused by our own Military to the vehicles requisitioned! But more of that later.

On the bus front, 1942 saw a reorganisation of the Tilling & BAT group to tidy up the investments of Thomas Tilling Ltd and the British Electric Traction Co, of which BAT was a subsidiary. Although most of the major bus companies in England and Wales were subsidiaries of Tilling & BAT, in practice either Tilling or BET had a dominant shareholding, and it was decided that two separate holding companies should be set up to reflect this, one run directly by Tilling, the other by BET. As part of this arrangement Southern Vectis came directly under Tilling control. Unlike the BET companies, those within the Tilling Group were subject to stringent restraints regarding vehicle policy and liveries. Bristol and Eastern Coach Works became the standard chassis and body manufacturers, whilst the group's subsidiaries generally adopted a livery of either red or green, with two cream bands on double-deckers and cream window surrounds on saloons; mudguards and wheels were black. Coaches were painted cream with red or green relief. Southern Vectis, not unnaturally, adopted the green version of the standard livery.

As has already been mentioned, many Southern Vectis vehicles had been requisitioned by the Ministry of Defence, and in total these amounted to very nearly a third of the entire fleet. Among those commandeered were all the AEC Regals, including the newest coaches, together with a number of Dennis Lancets and Aces and some older single-deckers. By 1942 Southern Vectis was feeling the need for additional vehicles to compensate for at least some of this deficit, and to help out three Regals with Harrington coach bodies (GO 1380/1, 1410) were loaned from Thomas Tilling of London, being joined in 1943 by a further three similar coaches (GN 1368/74/6); all had returned to the mainland by May 1944. Assistance was also provided by Wilts & Dorset Motor Services, which sent four Leyland Lions. Two, dating from 1929/30, had Leyland bus bodies (MW 4595, 7052), the remaining pair (WV 5861, 8166), new in 1934/5, having 32-seat Duple coach bodies; all were returned to Wilts & Dorset in 1945.

Bus production had officially ceased on the outbreak of war, although vehicles in the course of construction were completed. Thereafter manufacturers continued to produce vehicles by utilising parts from existing stocks; these were known as 'unfrozen', by virtue of the fact that the stored parts had been 'unfrozen' for use. When this supply of parts was exhausted

and it was realised that many operators were in desperate need of new vehicles the Ministry of Supply drew up specifications for a standard double- and single-deck bus that could be built at minimum cost in terms of both materials and labour. Aluminium could not be used, resulting in much heavier vehicles, and bodies were devoid of such niceties as double-curvature front and rear domes, which required the services of a skilled panel-beater. Opening windows were limited to one per side per deck, and seats were of slatted wood. Bedford was chosen as the manufacturer of single-deckers, producing its OWB model, a wartime version of its petrol-engined normal-control OB chassis. Guy Motors of Wolverhampton was appointed to produce double-deck chassis, adapting its Arab chassis for the purpose.

As the war progressed the specifications were relaxed, and other manufacturers were commissioned to build what became known as the 'utilities', both Bristol and Daimler being selected to build double-deck chassis. Although Bristol chassis found their way into the fleets of many operators that had not previously run them, they were also allocated to most Tilling fleets, where they

were warmly welcomed and generally the peacetime standard. However, although the Gardner 5LW and 6LW had been the standard power units for the Guy Arab since its introduction, they were not offered as an option for the utility Bristol, all wartime Bristol chassis being fitted with the 7.7-litre six-cylinder AEC A202 engine and thus classified K6A.

In 1944 Southern Vectis was allocated one utility Bristol double-decker, which materialised as 704 (DDL 688). Some sources state that the chassis was fitted with the standard AEC engine but that this was replaced by a Gardner 5LW on arrival at Newport. However, there were instances of operators' sending Gardner 5LWs to Bristol for building into new chassis, where such engines had been held as spares or removed from older vehicles. Thus a handful of wartime chassis was actually built as K5Gs, and DDL 688 could well have been one such. Whichever story is correct, it certainly had a 5LW engine by the time it entered service.

The choice of bodywork was also strictly limited, and initially two coachbuilders were allocated to build double-deck bodies on

The first utility bus delivered to Southern Vectis, in 1944, was Park Royal-bodied Bristol K6A 704 (DDL 688), seen postwar at Ryde in the company of Harrington-bodied Dennis Lancet 521 (DL 9711). The stringent wartime regulations dictated that there should be only one opening window on each side on each deck, although by the time this view was recorded the small original headlamps had been replaced with a pair of larger units. *Alan B. Cross*

In 1953 No 704 was fitted with a new lowbridge body by Eastern Coach Works. Looking like new on Ryde Esplanade on 16 September that year, it awaits passengers with a full set of blinds for route 8 to Bembridge, on the eastern side of the Isle of Wight. In this form 704 was to serve Southern Vectis until 1967, the chassis thus putting in a creditable 23 years. *J. H. Ashton*

The need for vehicles during World War 2 became desperate as buses either became time-expired or were requisitioned by the War Department. Southern Vectis thus undertook a limited programme of rebodying involving the Dennis Lancets of 1935; seen here in Newport, 516 (DL 9706) received a utility Eastern Coach Works body, with a protruding section covering the steering column. *Roy Marshall / East Pennine Traction Group*

Bristol chassis. Park Royal was chosen to build highbridge bodies, the Hampshire firm of Strachans being contracted to build the lowbridge version. No 704 received a highbridge Park Royal body to the standard 56-seat layout. Constructed from sub-standard materials, utility bodies were more often than not subject to rebuilding or replacement within a few years, and in 1951 704 was fitted with the lower PV2 postwar radiator and a new 55-seat lowbridge ECW body. With its Gardner engine it was then virtually indistinguishable from the standard postwar double-decker.

Between 1943 and 1946 eight of the Dennis Lances (with Harrington or Eastern Counties bodies) that had been requisitioned by the Ministry of Transport in 1941 were re-purchased by SVOC. They had suffered badly in the hands of the military, and six were in such poor condition that rebodying was the only option. (The other two, along with some non-requisitioned examples, would later be rebuilt by Margham.) Nos 501/2/6/14-6 were therefore despatched to Irthlingborough, Northants, whither ECW had been evacuated, and were given new 35-seat rear-entrance bodies. Whilst not selected to build bodies on new chassis, ECW had been given the task of rebodying older or war-damaged vehicles and, whilst these were ostensibly to utility specification they were generally to a much more relaxed design. The Southern Vectis examples, apart from a squared-off front dome and a sharply angled front dash, were of quite pleasing appearance, with well-rounded rear dome and radiused corners to the windows, showing more than a hint of the postwar design that was to follow.

Two further utility buses arrived on the island in 1944. The extra traffic generated by the Fleet Air Arm's occupation of the Puckpool Holiday Camp was such that Seaview Services was allocated two new Bedford OWB single-deckers. The 32-seat bodywork was built by Duple to Ministry of Supply specification, and whilst bonnet and wings were to Bedford's normal design,

the rest was distinctly austere, with virtually no curved surfaces. Delivered in October 1944, they were registered DDL 649/62.

June 1944 saw the D-Day landings in Normandy, providing a springboard from which the Allied Forces were able to liberate Western Europe — a task in which the Isle of Wight played no small part. Tests had been carried out as early as May 1942 on laying a pipeline in deep water, firstly in the River Medway and then in the Firth of Clyde. The eventual result of these tests was PLUTO (**P**ipe **L**ine **U**nder **T**he **O**cean); this traversed the island from Thorness Bay to Shanklin Chine, from where it crossed the English Channel on the seabed to Cherbourg, in northern France. Through the pipeline, considered to be one of the greatest feats of military engineering, were pumped millions of gallons of fuel, providing a critical supply to the Allied Forces.

The war in Europe ended in May 1945, and the following month saw the arrival of three more double-deckers at Nelson Road. This time there was no argument; they were Bristol K6As fitted with 7.7-litre AEC engines. The first, 705 (DDL 759), carried a highbridge Park Royal utility body, broadly similar to that on 704 but to a slightly more relaxed specification: there were more opening windows, and these were of the sliding rather than half-drop variety. The other two, 706/7 (DDL 764/5), had bodies by

◄ How to make an angular body look attractive. Standing at Ryde Esplanade *c*1945, Southern Vectis Bristol K6A/Park Royal utility 705 (DDL 759), complete with small headlamps and sliding window vents, looks well in the prewar livery of apple green and cream topped with dark-green roof. Note the ornate cast-iron box for road grit — so much a feature of days gone by — with menacing razor-tooth top to deter young climbers! *The Omnibus Society*

Southern Vectis received only four utility buses, the second Park Royal-bodied Bristol K type, delivered in 1945, being accompanied by a Duple-bodied pair. One of the latter was 707 (DDL 765), seen at Ryde Esplanade in April 1949. Records state that this bus and 705/6 were delivered with AEC engines, being re-engined in 1953 with the standard five-cylinder Gardner. Close scrutiny of the advertisement board reveals that on Whit Sunday one could watch the Silver Band or attend an orchestra performance. Judging by the upstairs window of 707 youths of the day also put their feet up on the front ledge. Some things never change! *Alan B. Cross*

Delivered in 1945 with a Duple utility body, Southern Vectis Bristol K 706 (DDL 764) was rebodied in 1953 with this lowbridge Eastern Coach Works version, giving it a new lease of life. When this photograph was taken in the late 1960s it was approaching the end of its 22 years' service with the company. *Malcolm Keeping*

Duple (which had by this time been authorised to build on Bristol chassis), and again these were to a relaxed design. Photographic evidence suggests that they were painted in prewar livery complete with lining-out but with the addition of a dark-green roof. In 1953 all three, fitted with low PV2 radiators and with their AEC engines replaced with Gardner 5LW units, would be sent to Lowestoft to receive new 55-seat lowbridge bodies.

Despite the new arrivals buses were still in short supply, and, to help out, three second-hand machines were purchased. The first of these (OV 8100), a Dennis Lancet with 32-seat body by AutoCellulose, was bought from City of Oxford Motor Services and given fleet number 526. The other two acquisitions were a little more unusual for the SVOC fleet, being Leyland Titan TD1 double-deckers purchased from Cardiff Corporation. No 708 (UH 7175), with lowbridge body, had been new in 1929, while 709 (TF 6821) had a highbridge body and dated from 1931; both had originally been Leyland demonstrators. In 1949 they had their Leyland petrol engines replaced by the ubiquitous Gardner 5LW, 'Covrad' radiators fitted to modernise their appearance and received new 55-seat lowbridge ECW bodywork to the Lowestoft builder's standard postwar design. The era of standardisation had arrived.

Acquisitions like this 1931 Leyland TD1 from Cardiff Corporation — one of nine such buses received by Southern Vectis in 1945 — indicated the desperate state of the operating industry after the cessation of World War 2. Having acquired a lowbridge Eastern Coach Works body in 1949, 708 (TF 6821) is seen here in Newport on a grim day in 1951. Note the starting handle, which would fall well short of today's Health & Safety standards! *Alan B. Cross*

This rear view of Leyland TD1/ECW rebody 708 (TF 6821) turning in Newport shows how well the type blended into the Southern Vectis fleet. The photograph was taken in July 1951, three years before withdrawal. Nowadays we bemoan the fact that every high street has the same shops, but note the presence here of Bateman's opticians, the Stead & Simpson shoe shop and Boots the chemists, all still around today. *Alan B. Cross*

The acquisition in 1945 from City of Oxford Motor Services of 526 (OV 8100), a 1932 Dennis Lancet with Auto Cellulose bodywork, was a logical move given the shortage of vehicles and the fact that this type of chassis was already familiar to Southern Vectis. Seen in cream coach livery on 29 July 1949, with driver in summer uniform and passengers disembarking, this trusty vehicle would remain in stock until 1951. *Alan B. Cross*

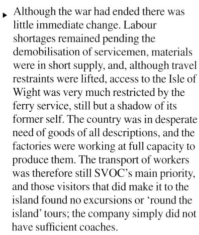

Delivered in 1946, Southern Vectis Bristol K5G 710 (DDL 985), with lowbridge ECW bodywork, was the first new double-decker to be delivered to the company after World War 2, at a time when operators were clamouring for new vehicles. One can almost hear the five-cylinder Gardner engine knocking as the bus rounds the corner on Ryde Esplanade. Note the uneasy match of rounded fixed windows and square-cornered sliders — a feature to be remedied on buses delivered in 1947. *W. J. Haynes / Southdown Enthusiasts' Club*

Although the war had ended there was little immediate change. Labour shortages remained pending the demobilisation of servicemen, materials were in short supply, and, although travel restraints were lifted, access to the Isle of Wight was very much restricted by the ferry service, still but a shadow of its former self. The country was in desperate need of goods of all descriptions, and the factories were working at full capacity to produce them. The transport of workers was therefore still SVOC's main priority, and those visitors that did make it to the island found no excursions or 'round the island' tours; the company simply did not have sufficient coaches.

The bus fleet was in a pretty sorry state. Years of hard work and poor maintenance had taken its toll, and the appearance of the fleet was not helped by the number of vehicles in drab overall grey or brown, while those that had escaped the ignominy of camouflage were badly in need of repainting. Underneath the paintwork the bodywork and mechanics were in urgent need of attention.

Obviously bus operators throughout the country, in the same position, were clamouring for new vehicles and the rebuilding of existing stock. The major bus builders were affected by the same shortages of staff and materials and were unable to cope with the onslaught. This resulted in many operators' having to take chassis types that were non-standard to their fleets and from a plethora of bodybuilders. Firms previously engaged in building lorries, high-class cars or even aircraft saw a lucrative opening and turned their hands to building buses and coaches. Such names as Mann Egerton, Windover, Portsmouth Aviation and Gurney Nutting began to be seen on coachbuilders' nameplates.

Southern Vectis was lucky. The Tilling Group, it seemed, looked after its own, and Bristol and ECW appeared able to fulfil

its needs, even though they were building for operators outside the Group. Thus in 1946 five new buses were delivered to Nelson Road.

Nos 710/1 (DDL 985/6) were K5Gs with 55-seat lowbridge bodies by ECW, being to the second version of that concern's postwar design with six sliding vents per side. After the first 50 postwar 'deckers vents were fitted to all main bays. The vents themselves were square-cornered and were fitted above fixed panes with radiused corners. These and the push-out vents at the front were painted in the main body colour.

The lowbridge layout was now adopted as standard, and all new 'deckers until the advent of the Lodekka would be to this design. Hitherto double-deckers, being of highbridge construction, had been limited to the Ryde–Newport–Cowes services, which encountered no low bridges. The steady influx of lowbridge buses would enable other heavily trafficked routes to be double-decked, notably the busy 16 from Ryde to Shanklin via

The first single-decker delivered to Southern Vectis postwar was Bristol L5G/ECW 830 (EDL 15), seen at Ryde Esplanade. Like their double-deck cousins delivered the same year the Ls had squared sliding windows but somehow did not look so incongruous with the rounded edges to the fixed windows and were thus quite attractive vehicles. *The Omnibus Society*

Brading, which passed under two low bridges at Moreton and Lake. Later the route would be extended to Ventnor and Blackgang, becoming one of the island's busiest services.

The remaining new vehicles of 1946 were 829-31 (EDL 14-16), Bristol L5Gs with ECW 35-seat bodies. These too were to the immediate postwar design and had the same kind of windows as the 'deckers.

There were also two second-hand acquisitions at this time. One was a Dennis Lancet, 527 (PJ 5032), which came from Fountain Coaches. This had a 32-seat body of uncertain make, but as the bus had started life as a Dennis demonstrator the likelihood is that Dennis also built the body. The second was another 1929 Leyland Titan TD1, this time from Hants & Dorset. Numbered 712 (TK 1854), it was fitted with a new lowbridge Beadle body immediately before crossing the Solent, replacing its original outside staircase one. It also received a Gardner 5LW engine, probably at the same time.

Acquired by Southern Vectis in 1946 from Fountain Coaches was this 1932 Dennis Lancet, 527 (PJ 5032), seen in Ryde Esplanade station yard. Despite its antiquated appearance it would serve the company for three years, not being withdrawn until 1949. *The Omnibus Society*

29

Given the ground-breaking nature of the Leyland Titan TD1 chassis when introduced in the late 1920s it is perhaps curious that the type should have taken nearly two decades to reach the Isle of Wight. That they appeared at all was due to the desperate shortage of suitable vehicles, but they would prove to be good workhorses. Acquired from Hants & Dorset Motor Services in 1946 and rebodied by Beadle of Dartford in August of that year, 712 (TK 1854) is seen in St James's Square, Newport. *Michael Rooum*

After the make-do-and-mend years of the war and the immediate postwar period the 1947 intake of new ECW-bodied Bristol K5Gs must have seemed a blessing for the engineering staff at Southern Vectis. Basking serenely in the sun at Yarmouth on 18 September 1953, 721 (EDL 657) has already had its nearside destination screen overpainted. Withdrawn in 1964, it is happily now part of the Isle of Wight Bus & Coach Museum collection. *J. H. Aston*

To help out with coaching requirements, two Thornycrofts — a 'Hardy' and a 'Dainty' — were loaned from the Caledonian Omnibus Co of Dumfries, spending the summer of 1946 on the Isle of Wight before returning north of the border.

'Worst for 200 years' said the headlines, referring to the winter of 1947, which did little to help a nation struggling to recover from six years of war, and rationing and shortages were compounded by arctic conditions and power cuts. However, not all was doom and gloom, for in the spring another seven double-deckers, 713-9 (EDL 17-23), were received by Southern Vectis, to be followed at the end of the year by a further four, 720-3 (EDL 656-9). These were the now standard combination of Bristol K5G chassis and 55-seat lowbridge ECW body, differing from the previous year's intake only in having aluminium sliding vents with rounded corners fitted inside the

window pans, a design of window that was to remain ECW's standard until around 1980. The front push-out vents were also of unpainted aluminium. These much-needed buses enabled double-deck operation to be expanded, service 10 from Newport to Ventnor via Blackwater and Niton being a candidate for conversion.

Also delivered over the course of the summer were six Bedford OBs with 29-seat Duple coach bodies, numbered 208-13 (EDL 637-42). Introduced in 1939 but replaced by the OWB during the war, the OB was reintroduced in October 1945 and rapidly became the most popular choice for the majority of independent bus and coach operators; in fact no small operator could be considered worthy of his salt unless there was a Bedford OB in his fleet. The OB was of normal-control (bonneted) design with a 3.5-litre petrol engine, and the 29-seat Duple Vista body was the most common, although other coachbuilders did body the type. Memories of the OB are of squeaking springs and, in later years, petrol fumes! Nevertheless they were very useful workhorses

for both bus and coach use, their small size enabling them to negotiate winding country lanes and narrow streets alike.

The Caledonian Omnibus Co again helped out during the summer by lending Southern Vectis two Thornycroft Daintys with 20-seat Brush bodywork.

Clement Attlee's Labour Government, as part of its nationalisation agenda, had introduced the 1947 Transport Act, which came into force in January 1948. The British Transport Commission was formed to nationalise the railways together with their interests in road haulage and road passenger transport, the ultimate objective being the creation of a fully integrated transport system (although this was to be frustrated by a change of Government in 1951). Thus the Tilling Group was acquired by the BTC, and Southern Vectis became a nationalised company, although there was no outward sign of change. Bristol and Eastern Coach Works also came under Government control and were no longer allowed to supply non-State-owned companies.

Nowadays the Duple-bodied Bedford OB is held in great affection, but in the late 1940s and early '50s they were 'ten a penny'. How useful they must have been on the narrow roads of the Isle of Wight. Southern Vectis 208 (EDL 637), dating from 1947, takes in the sun whilst parked up on a private-hire duty. *W. J. Haynes / Southdown Enthusiasts' Club*

A Southern Vectis Bedford OB/Duple, 221 (GDL 796) of 1950, doing what it did best, carrying a party of excursion passengers at Alum Bay. To extend their lives these worthy machines would later be fitted with Perkins diesel engines, being used thereafter on stage-carriage work until their final demise in 1963. *Glyn Kraemer-Johnson collection*

By this time, although there were still shortages, and rationing remained in force, life was gradually returning to normal, and public transport was flourishing. After six years of hardship, danger and uncertainty the British people wanted to enjoy themselves. Theatres and cinemas were thriving, the fortnight's annual holiday was taken in Britain and there were works outings and day trips, invariably taken by coach. The level of car ownership was still low, and the journey to the holiday resort would be by train or express coach. Once there, the area would be explored by bus or by day or half-day coach tours. It was a time of long queues at bus stops, of standing loads and relief buses.

Deliveries of new vehicles remained very standardised for the rest of the decade. A further 10 Bedford/Duple OBs were received to help with SVOC's coaching needs, whilst double-deckers were all lowbridge ECW-bodied K5Gs, two of which had a particularly interesting start to life.

Not surprisingly London Transport had suffered particularly badly during the war, and its fleet was drastically in need of replacement. Delivery of new vehicles was slow, so to help out the Tilling Group agreed that 25% of its new double-deckers should be diverted to London. As might be imagined, the Tilling companies were not overjoyed at losing their new buses, whilst London Transport drivers did not take readily to driving Bristols, and their passengers certainly didn't appreciate the lowbridge layout to which most of them were built. Nevertheless Southern Vectis 729/30 (FDL 297/8) were delivered direct to London Transport, with which they worked from Harrow Weald and Nunhead garages on routes 140, 230 and 63. They finally arrived on the island in November 1949 after nine months' hard work in the capital.

On 1 June 1950 legislation was introduced increasing the maximum permitted length of double-deckers to 27ft and of single-deckers to 30ft, the maximum width of both being increased

This rear view of Southern Vectis Bristol K5G 724 (FDL 292) of 1948 shows just how low the lowbridge ECW body is configured, with long seats for four across the width of the bus and the sunken gangway on the offside of the upper deck. The location is the Bull Ring, Brading, in the east of the island, this tranquil scene reflecting village life. The indicator post fulfils three functions: as a direction post, lamp post and bus stop, the flag for which is almost out of sight for other than upper-deck passengers!
A. D. Packer

In 1948/9 came the next intake of lowbridge ECW-bodied Bristol K5Gs. However, of these 729/30 were delivered direct to London Transport to alleviate that operator's vehicle shortages. No 730 (FDL 298) is seen on route 63 passing Farringdon station in July 1949. Not until November of that year would the pair be received by their intended owner, after more than 12 months' arduous work in the capital.
Alan B. Cross

33

After the relaxation of wartime restrictions the Tilling Group reverted to its preferred Bristol/ECW chassis/body combination. A K5G delivered early in 1950, 733 (FDL 985) would be withdrawn nearly 15 years later, in late 1964. This view at Ryde Esplanade was recorded in the early 1960s, at which time the pier in the background was still host to steam trains. The mainland is just visible in the far distance. *Howard Butler*

Parked in the middle of Newport bus station is lowbridge Bristol K5G/ECW 729 (FDL 297). The Autovac for the fuel system is clearly visible on the nearside front bulkhead, while the destination/number display has been rebuilt in a 'T' layout more suited to simpler destination blinds. To its left can be seen Bristol L5G 835. *Howard Butler*

from 7ft 6in to 8ft. Chassis- and bodybuilders adapted their models to meet the new dimensions, and, in the case of Bristol, the lengthened K type became the 'KS' which, rather confusingly, stood for '**K** type **S**hort'. The reason for this was that Bristol was expecting a further increase in overall length and was thus ready to produce the 'KL'. In the event this never happened, at least in the lifetime of the K. The 8ft-wide version was known quite logically as the KSW. ECW increased the dimensions of its standard bodywork but, in the case of the double-decker, also gave it quite a radical face-lift. Although its ancestry was clearly visible, the body was now of four-bay construction, with a small 'quarter' bay (albeit unglazed) at the rear of the lower deck. The front profile was slightly more curved, the lower edges of the windscreen and front bulkhead window were curved rather than angled, and there was a slight 'bulge' beneath the windscreen, which harked back to the prewar design.

The last K5Gs for Southern Vectis, 738/9 (GDL 711/2), were amongst the last to be built with the old-style body and were followed immediately by three KS5Gs, 740-2 (GDL 713-5), SVOC having decided that in view of the island's roads it would be prudent to stay with the 7ft 6in width.

As far as Bristol's single-deck range was concerned, the 30ft chassis was designated 'LL' and the 8ft-wide version 'LWL'. The standard ECW body was lengthened and widened but otherwise remained unchanged, making it if anything even more handsome. Southern Vectis took three of the LL types with 39-seat bodywork, numbering them 832-4 (GDL 716-8). The islanders, it seems, love to give nicknames to their buses, and the Bristol LLs were always known as 'Long Toms'.

The late 1940s saw the dawning of the 'Hi-de-Hi' era — the heyday of the holiday camps — which was good news for the island's bus and coach operators and in particular

A photograph revealing that the only way into Ventnor is down! With the exception of the street furniture the scene can have changed little since the late 19th century — other than being enhanced by the presence of 736 (GDL 434), a Bristol K5G with lowbridge ECW bodywork! Also deserving of attention are the early style of 'NO ENTRY' sign and the Morris Minor 1000 parked at the side of the road. *Howard Butler*

Numerically the last of seven Bristol K5Gs delivered in 1950, 739 (GDL 712) was less than three years old when seen on 27 June 1953 at Ryde Esplanade station. The elderly lady at the front of the lower saloon looks on in amusement at the photographer — but how grateful we are to him for recording this scene. *J. H. Aston*

The same bus at Newport bus station in the mid-1960s. By this time it had fallen from grace somewhat, part of the 'via' blind on the destination box having been blanked off for the route number. Note also the car park, complete with 1960s Vauxhall Victors, a Ford 100E and an early Morris Minor. Newport bus station would close in 2005, consigning views such as this to history. *Howard Butler*

Seaview Services, which company's route served the Puckpool Holiday Camp. Since its wartime OWBs, Seaview had added six Bedford OBs — four with Duple coach bodies and two with Mulliner bus bodies for stage-carriage work. A second-hand Bedford WTB dating from 1937 was acquired in 1950 to supplement the coach fleet. By this time passenger loadings on the Ryde–Seaview service were proving too much for the small-capacity Bedfords, and in May of that year two Leyland Titan double-deckers with Leyland's own lowbridge bodywork, resplendent in the company's livery of red and two-tone green, were delivered to the Seafield garage. GDL 764/5, being of type PD2/1, were to the old dimensions of 7ft 6in x 26ft 0in and were amongst the last of the type to be built before new longer and wider chassis became standard. They were also amongst the last to have the immediate postwar body design, what has come to be known as the 'Farington' style being introduced to meet the new dimensions. GDL 765 would be withdrawn in 1963, but GDL 764

was to soldier on until 1971, when it was sold for use as a garden shed; fortunately it was rescued and has since been restored to its former glory.

Southern Vectis too was finding it difficult to cope with the ever-increasing levels of traffic, and to help out Wilts & Dorset loaned six Leyland TD1s dating from 1931. Given fleet numbers 743-8, these had various UF 7xxx registrations, indicating their origins with Southdown Motor Services (the Brighton connection again!); they had passed to Wilts & Dorset in 1939, since when they had gained Brush utility bodies and had their Leyland petrol engines replaced by the ubiquitous Gardner 5LW. They remained with Southern Vectis for almost two years, returning to the mainland in December 1951.

By now Britain was getting back on her feet. The next few years would see the Festival of Britain and the Coronation of HM Queen Elizabeth II . . . and would undoubtedly represent the heyday of the British bus.

No book on the Isle of Wight's buses would be complete without a mention of the well-known Seaview Services route from Ryde to Seaview.
In the face of Nationalisation after the war the service survived, seemingly against all odds. Pictured on 27 August 1970 is all-Leyland Titan PD2/1 GDL 764, which was to outlast its twin by eight years. The location is the Duver Toll Road, the use of which required that an extra penny be added to the fare! *Alan Snatt*

Despite showing scars from overhanging branches Seaview Services GDL 764 still sparkles outside the Seaview garage in July 1971; note in particular the gleaming front wheel-hub ring. Thankfully this bus survives in preservation on the island and regularly attends rallies and running days. *Dave Brown*

So many photographs exist of Seaview Services all-Leyland Titan PD2 GDL 764, which survives in preservation, that one almost forgets its twin, GDL 765, seen here at Ryde Esplanade shortly before withdrawal in 1963. *Glyn Kraemer-Johnson collection*

The early history of the Southern Vectis company is linked in many respects to that of Southdown Motor Services, so it was perhaps appropriate that after the war six ex-Southdown Leyland Titan TD1s would be received on long-term loan from Wilts & Dorset in 1950. They were interesting beasts, having been fitted with lowbridge utility bodywork by Brush in 1944 and had their original Leyland petrol engines replaced postwar by Gardner 5LW units. Although they were given Southern Vectis fleetnames, careful study of this photograph of 745 (UF 7396), taken in July 1951, reveals the Wilts & Dorset legal lettering. The Vernon's advertisement appears to have faded somewhat, leaving contemporary football fans in some doubt as to where they should send their pools coupons! *Alan B. Cross*

Basking in glorious sunshine outside the Sandown Hotel on 26 July 1949 is Enterprise of Newport AJH 870, an Auto Cellulose-bodied Dennis Lancet dating from 1935. Note the steering box and mechanism below the offside headlamp and the bald tyre, such was the scarcity of replacements after the lean war years. Within two years Enterprise would be taken over by Southern Vectis, AJH 870 being allocated fleet number 526 and lasting another three years before withdrawal in 1954. *Alan B. Cross*

The Skylon, the Dome of Discovery, the Festival Hall and a Bristol Lodekka. All were features of the 1951 Festival of Britain. This was a chance for Britain to show off her achievements and, whilst the country still had a long way to go to recover fully from the war, the mood of the people was one of optimism.

At this time there were still a number of independent stage-carriage operators on the Isle of Wight, but by 1959 only one would remain. The first to go was Enterprise of Newport, which operated two services between Newport and Sandown, via Arreton and Newchurch. The undertaking was acquired by Southern Vectis in June 1951, bringing six vehicles into the fleet. Of particular interest were two ex-Reading Guy Arabs with lowbridge utility bodies by Strachans; they were numbered 900/1 (BRD 754, 816). Also taken into stock were 526 (AJH 870), a Dennis Lancet, and a trio of Bedfords — OWBs 32/3 (DDL 532, 706) and OB 34 (GDL 226) — with Duple bus bodywork, of which the last, dating from 1949, would remain

with SVOC until 1963, being a frequent performer on the rural Alverstone service.

Deliveries of new vehicles to Southern Vectis were much as before, more KS5Gs, 749-58 (HDL 263-72), and LL5Gs, 835-43 (HDL 279-87), being delivered over the winter of 1951/2. Different, however, were three new heavyweight coaches. Since the end of the war ECW's only offering for the coach market had been the 'express' or dual-purpose version of the standard single-deck bus body, operators requiring something a little more luxurious having to turn to other coachbuilders such as Duple and Beadle. In 1950 ECW had introduced a 'proper' coach body which, although retaining the traditional Bristol radiator, featured a full front. With the increase in maximum dimensions the design was modified to incorporate the extra length and width, and at the same time the radiator was concealed behind an ornamental grille with an elliptical surround. Their extra length led to these coaches' being nicknamed 'Queen Marys' long before the epithet was applied to a certain operator's Leyland PD3 double-deckers . . . The three for Southern Vectis were mounted on Bristol LWL6B chassis, utilising Bristol's own six-cylinder AVW engine, and were numbered 300-2 (HDL 182-4), starting another new series, this time for full-size coaches. Unfortunately the age of the underfloor-engined coach had dawned, and, like so many front-engined coaches of the time, they were outdated as soon as they entered service. Nevertheless they gave 10 years' service.

Having taken delivery of 8ft-wide coaches, Southern Vectis finally decided that double-deckers to the same width would be acceptable, and thus 10 KSW5Gs arrived in the shape of 759-68 (JDL 33-42), their delivery being spread over the course of a year from May 1951 to May 1952. Their extra width aside they were little different from the KS-types, and to this writer it always seemed strange that, bearing in mind the extra size of these buses and the hilly terrain of the Isle of Wight, Southern Vectis stuck doggedly to the 5LW engine, the 6LW or Bristol AVW being much more popular choices for the KSW chassis.

During 1950/1 Bristol, along with most other major chassis manufacturers, had developed a new single-deck chassis with the engine placed on its side beneath the floor. This allowed the

Acquired with the Enterprise business in June 1951, Southern Vectis Bedford OB 207 (GDL 226) is seen at Newport bus station *c*1960 on local service 15A. Note the four-circle emblem on the radiator, signifying that the vehicle has been re-engined with a Perkins diesel unit. *Glyn Kraemer-Johnson collection*

Also inherited from Enterprise was this lowbridge Strachans-bodied Guy Arab, 700 (BRD 816). New to Reading Corporation in 1943, it was to remain in the Southern Vectis fleet until 1956. In this view, recorded in Newport, the passengers seem bemused that anyone should contemplate taking such a photograph! *A. M. Wright / Southdown Enthusiasts' Club*

When this photograph was taken in the early 1960s Ventnor boasted a rail connection as well as an efficient bus service provided by Southern Vectis. Eastern Coach Works-bodied Bristol KS5G 749 (HDL 263) approaches the town hall on route 16 to Blackgang; note the 'lazy' destination display. *Howard Butler*

An early 1960s view of lowbridge Bristol KS5G/ECW 752 (HDL 266) of 1951 parked up at Ryde Esplanade. Visible in the background are the Solent and the city of Portsmouth. In days gone by the Solent witnessed many more naval ships plying to and fro on active service for their country, although Portsmouth remains home to the Royal Navy. *Howard Butler*

Another favourite with enthusiasts is the postwar Eastern Coach Works-bodied Bristol L type, and this view of LL5G 835 (HDL 279) at Newport bus station in the early 1960s should help to explain why. The advertisement on the side does little to enhance its appearance but was necessary to supplement falling revenue from passengers. Note the delightful early-postwar Vauxhall behind.
Howard Butler

The venue for this early-1960s view is Sandown's Sandringham Hotel, where Bristol LL5G/ECW 842 (HDL 286) is seen heading away from the seafront. The bus still looks pristine after 10 years or so in service.
Howard Butler

43

The underfloor-engined chassis was already on the horizon when the full-fronted Bristol LWL/ECW coach became available to BTC companies, and only a few were produced. Although the body style represented a leap forward they always appeared to be very sad-looking vehicles, as evident from this view at Alum Bay of Southern Vectis 301 (HDL 183), delivered in 1951. The batch of three would last barely 10 years, being withdrawn *en bloc* in October 1961. *Glyn Kraemer-Johnson collection*

In the 1950s the Eastern Coach Works design team at Lowestoft got it right every time, as exemplified by the coach body built on the underfloor-engined Bristol LS. Delivered in 1952, the initial batch for Southern Vectis had six-cylinder Gardner engines. Seen resting between duties on the 'Round the Island' tour is 304 (JDL 45). *Alan B. Cross*

whole of the floor space to be used for seating, thereby increasing capacity. It also permitted the entrance to be positioned ahead of the front wheels — something that was to become very important later in the decade, although it was not immediately adopted by all coachbuilders. The Tilling Group had for some time been looking at the possibility of a lightweight single-decker, and the Bristol LS ('**L**ight **S**aloon') fulfilled this requirement as well; of semi-integral construction, it made extensive use of light alloys, being thus considerably lighter than its contemporaries.

Unlike the 'Queen Mary', ECW's coach body for the LS was a true classic. Businesslike but extremely handsome, it featured a straight waistrail curving downwards at the front, an outward-opening car-type door ahead of the front wheels, standard ECW

sliding vents and a front adorned only by a winged motif, which on later versions incorporated the Bristol badge. Its simplicity was striking when compared to some of the bulbous, over-embellished American-car-influenced horrors being produced at the time.

To say that Southern Vectis was an early user of the LS would be something of an understatement, the company taking five LS6G coaches powered by Gardner's 6HLW engine (the horizontal version of the 6LW) in the summer and autumn of 1952. They were numbered 303-7 (JDL 44-8), 303 actually having the first production LS chassis. JDL 43 did not arrive until some the following year. A further LS, it was powered by the ever-faithful five-cylinder Gardner and fitted with a

The Bristol/ECW LS coach was arguably the most attractive of all underfloor-engined designs of the early 1950s. In full coach livery, Southern Vectis 307 (JDL 48) stands at Ryde Esplanade on an horrendously wet day in the early 1960s; note the umbrellas in the background and that even the excursion boards have been stacked up in despair! No 307 would remain with Southern Vectis until 1971, spending its last days as a bus, renumbered 857. *Howard Butler*

Despite taking no fewer than 11 ECW-bodied Bristol LS coaches Southern Vectis received only one bus version. Delivered in 1953, 844 (JDL 43) had the standard (for Southern Vectis buses) five-cylinder Gardner engine and would last 17 years before withdrawal. Our photograph shows it inside Shanklin garage, itself now long gone. *Photobus*

45-seat ECW bus body, again to a functional and businesslike design. Numbered 844, it was, for some reason, the only LS bus ever bought by the company.

The year 1952 also saw the beginning of the desecration of the island's railway network, with the closure of the line from Merstone to Ventnor West. This was not a closure that could be criticised — the line had never been well patronised and had been worked by two four-wheel coaches on a push-pull basis — but the following year saw the abandonment of the Newport–Freshwater line (originally the Freshwater, Newport & Yarmouth Railway) together with the branch from Brading to Bembridge. Southern Vectis introduced a replacement bus service for the latter and increased frequencies on its services from Newport to West Wight. It was the beginning of the end and something that would have considerable effect on the island's bus operators.

More KSW5Gs came into the SVOC fleet in 1953 as 769-73 (JDL 719-23), together with six more LS coaches, 308-13 (JDL 756-61). Of the latter 309-13 were LS6Bs, 308 alone having a Gardner 6HLW; it subsequently transpired that this vehicle should have been delivered to the Lincolnshire Road Car Co, and after just four months it was sent north-eastwards in exchange for KBE 179, the Bristol-engined coach that should have been delivered to Southern Vectis in the first place! It took the same fleet number of 308.

Mention has already been made of the lowbridge body design, with its awkward sunken side gangway. With most of its customers requiring low-height buses, Bristol had as far back as 1948 started work on a revolutionary design that materialised as the Lodekka. Without

Seen working a tour to the Needles, Bristol LS6B/ECW coach 308 (KBE 179) had a confused history inasmuch as it was intended for Southern Vectis but ended up being delivered to the Lincolnshire Road Car Co before finding its way to the Isle of Wight; in exchange Southern Vectis sent its original 308 (JDL 756), an LS6G, to Lincolnshire, and the confusion was undone, although the registrations remained unchanged.
Photobus

becoming too technical but at the same time not wishing to make light of an important landmark in the development of the bus, the basic idea was that by using a drop-centre rear axle, the transmission shaft could be offset to run near the offside of the chassis. This allowed for a slightly sunken gangway (by about 2in) in the centre of the lower deck, which, in turn, permitted a normal (central) gangway on the upper deck. The overall height was maintained at 13ft 6in unladen, the same as that of the traditional lowbridge bus.

Two prototype Lodekkas were built in 1949 and 1950, the second of which appeared at the Festival of Britain in 1951. In 1953 a further six pre-production buses were built, one of which (chassis number 100003) was delivered to Hants & Dorset as its 1337 (LRU 67). During the summer of 1953 this bus was loaned to Southern Vectis for evaluation purposes, as a result of which no fewer than 21 were ordered. All were delivered during April and May 1954, being numbered 500-20 (JDL 996-9, KDL 1, 401-16). They featured the long radiator common to the early Lodekkas and were classified LD6G, the company having finally decided to standardise on the Gardner 6LW. They were fitted with luggage racks over the rear wheel arches, reducing the

seating capacity to 54 from the usual 60. Another 20 Lodekkas, with a mixture of long and short radiator grilles, followed in 1955 as 521-40 (LDL 720-39).

The Bristol LS coaches of which Southern Vectis now had a comfortably sized fleet were ideal for longer tours and express work. However, for a local doddle round the island SVOC found the Bedford/Duple combination both cheaper and more suitable. Something larger than the OB was required, so in 1955 three Bedford SBO full size coaches were bought, the 'O' (for 'oil') indicating that they were diesel-powered. They were fitted with 38-seat Duple bodies of the type then being supplied to small coach operators in their hundreds and incorporating what became known as the 'butterfly' grille. Following on from the OBs, they were numbered 224-6 (LDL 626-8) and would be joined the following year by a further four, 231-4 (MDL 752/3, 818/9).

Seaview Services had also been buying Bedfords but in 1954 decided a back-up vehicle was needed for the Ryde–Seaview service. Bearing in mind its two all-Leyland PD2s it came as a surprise when a prewar AEC Regent arrived at Seafield Garage. CDK 209 had originated with Rochdale Corporation and carried a 57-seat highbridge body by Cravens of Sheffield.

Southern Vectis's first Bristol Lodekkas, delivered in 1954, must have been an absolute blessing for passengers on the Isle of Wight — no more crunching of heads on the ceiling! Numerically the second to be taken into stock, LD6G 501 (JDL 997), with full destination display, is seen on layover, showing the scars of battle on its nearside front wing. *Glyn Kraemer-Johnson collection*

A case of two for the price of one as Bristol LD6G 506 (KDL 402) of 1954 passes SUL4A 846 (459 ADL) on its way to Seaview. Fitted with a four-cylinder Albion engine, the Bristol SU was a lightweight type suited to rural routes, Southern Vectis taking a batch of eight in 1963. The bus stop, listing to starboard, appears to have been given a 'helping hand'! *Alan B. Cross*

Bound for Ryde, Southern Vectis Bristol LD6G 523 (LDL 722) of 1955 pauses by the Post Office in the village of Brading. Vehicles of this batch had a mix of long and short radiator grilles, this bus having one of the latter; note also the disc fitted to the rear wheel, enhancing the vehicle's appearance but no doubt a pain for the company's engineering staff. Although the photograph is undated, some clue can be gleaned from the fact that, according to the advertisement, the Medina 'Film Theatre' in Newport was screening *Love Story*, 'chosen for the Royal Film Performance 1971'. *Alan B. Cross*

The Bedford SB with Duple coachwork was as popular with the small operators as was its predecessor, the OB, but in the main was not favoured by major operators, which tended to prefer heavyweight chassis. Southern Vectis, however, was an exception to the rule, on account of the geography of the Isle of Wight and the limited mileage undertaken by its vehicles. Photographed at Ryde Esplanade, 231 (MDL 752), a Duple-bodied SBO delivered in 1956, had the small coach park to itself. *Alan B. Cross*

Seaview Motor Services was the 'other' operator of double-deck buses on the Isle of Wight. In carrying the crowds its well-known all-Leyland PD2s were assisted by Cravens-bodied AEC Regent CDK 209, which originally saw service in the Lancashire town of Rochdale but is seen in the late 1950s at Ryde Esplanade. The bodywork was no stranger to these parts, for over the water in Portsmouth was a large fleet of Cravens-bodied AEC trolleybuses that would survive until the early 1960s. *D. Clark*

This was undoubtedly the golden age of bus travel. Car ownership was still relatively low, foreign holidays were out of reach for the majority, and the cinema and theatre remained the main forms of entertainment. Bus operators were making hay while the sun shone, and Southern Vectis was no exception.

During 1955/6 another four operators were acquired. The first of these was Groves of Cowes, bringing with it licences to operate excursions from Cowes and a fleet of four postwar Bedfords — three OBs and an SB, all with Duple bodies. Next came the Shanklin Esplanade–Luccombe service of Bartlett's Garage Ltd, although no vehicles were included in the deal. This was followed by the stage-carriage services of Shotter's of Brighstone; again no vehicles were involved. Finally, in June 1956, the long-established business of Nash's Luxury Coaches of Ventnor was acquired. Included with tours and express licences were the office and garage in Pier Street, Ventnor, and five coaches, comprising two Duple-bodied Dennis Lancets, two Whitson-bodied Crossleys and a Commer Avenger with Harrington coachwork; all were taken into the SVOC fleet (numbered 100-4), although they lasted with the company for only three or four years. This spate of takeovers left Seaview Services as the island's sole independent stage-carriage operator—a situation probably safeguarded by its exclusive right to use the Duver toll road.

Waistcoats and flat caps were still common attire in the early 1950s, when Bartlett's Duple-bodied Bedford OB plied its trade on the Shanklin–Luccombe route. CTL 67 is seen leaving Shanklin shortly before the service passed to Southern Vectis. *Roy Marshall/ East Pennine Traction Group*

When the business of B. Groves of Cowes was acquired by Southern Vectis in 1955 HDL 570, a Duple-bodied Bedford SB dating from 1951, fitted in well with the latter's own fleet of Bedfords. Pictured in cream livery as Southern Vectis 230, it would see service until 1960. *Alan B. Cross*

51

Acquired by Southern Vectis in June 1956 was the business of Nash, Ventnor, which brought with it a varied fleet. Included was this handsome Whitson-bodied Crossley — a make commonplace in its native Lancashire but seldom seen in the South of England. GDL 32 duly became Southern Vectis 102, in which guise it is seen at Ryde Esplanade. *W. J. Haynes / Southdown Enthusiasts' Club*

Harrington-bodied Commer Avenger HDL 304 was new in 1951 to Nash Coaches of Ventnor and, when that company was acquired by Southern Vectis in 1956, was taken into the latter's fleet as No 104, surviving until 1960. The ladies' fashions evident in this view at Ryde Esplanade date the photograph to the late 1950s. *D. Clark*

New to Nash of Ventnor in 1947, Dennis Lancet III EDL 715, with
handsome Duple coachwork, was numbered 100 when acquired by
Southern Vectis, being seen thus at Ryde. Despite a slightly old-fashioned
appearance, created by the chassis' distinctive high radiator, it would give
the company three years' valuable service, not being withdrawn until 1959.
D. Clark

In 1955 Southern Vectis acquired from Bristol Tramways 14 Bristol K5Gs, with highbridge bodywork variously by BBW (Bristol's own coachbuilding facility), ECW and Beadle. Pictured in St James's Square, Newport, is 775 (FHT 811), with BBW body; behind, facilitating comparison with the lowbridge ECW style, is native KSW5G 765 (JDL 39) of 1953. *D. Clark / Southdown Enthusiasts' Club*

Another of the Bristol K5Gs received from Bristol Tramways was ECW-bodied 787 (GAE 498), seen in Newport. Already 14 years old when acquired, it would see only three years' service on the Isle of Wight but provided valuable cover pending the arrival of new vehicles. Note the route number slotted beneath the destination screen. *D. Clark*

The year 1954 had seen the closure of the Newport–Sandown railway line, again bringing increased traffic to Southern Vectis. Despite the influx of new Lodekkas the company still found itself short of double-deckers and, as a stopgap, 14 Bristol K5Gs dating from 1939-41 were purchased from Bristol Tramways. Thirteen, with various FHT, GAE and GHT registrations, had highbridge 56-seat bodywork by either ECW or Bristol's own bodybuilding facility (BBW), the odd one out being GHU 489, which had a lowbridge Beadle body. All retained their single-aperture destination screens but were fitted with brackets (on the waistrail above the canopy) into which were slotted small metal plates bearing the route number. The use of highbridge buses was becoming less of a problem, for, with the closure of railway lines, many of the low bridges were being demolished.

A larger fleet meant increased facilities. Construction had started in 1955 of a new Central Works at Nelson Road, Newport, which was opened in February 1956, while in June of the same year a new bus station/garage was opened in Landguard Road, Shanklin. A new bus station for Newport was also in the pipeline, but it would be 1962 before this became operational.

In 1956/7 two more Bristol K5Gs dating from 1939/40 with lowbridge ECW bodies were acquired, this time from Hants & Dorset, these being 788/9 (AFX 757, APR 426).

For the rest of the decade new vehicles consisted largely of LD6G Lodekkas and Bedford/Duple coaches, although the 1959 and 1960 coaches were of type SB8 and had bodies to an

updated design which, to the authors' eyes, was not nearly as attractive as its predecessor. The 1959 Lodekkas, 560-4 (SDL 265-9), were fitted with hopper windows instead of the usual sliders and with fewer of them, although they were also fitted to the front upper-deck windows; these latter were retained, but the side vents were later replaced by the usual eight sliding vents per side. A little variety was added in 1958, however, when a new vehicle type entered the fleet.

The LS single-deck chassis had proved popular, but by 1957 the general trend was away from integral construction. Bristol therefore decided to introduce a new single-decker with a conventional chassis completely separate from the body structure. ECW updated its body designs to suit the new chassis, which, although only about 3cwt heavier than the LS, was designated 'MW' ('**M**edium **W**eight'). Production of the bus version began in earnest at the end of 1957, the first coaches taking to the road in February 1958. In the spring of that year Southern Vectis received its first MWs in the shape of two 39-seat coaches, 314/5 (PDL 514/5). They were of type MW6G, with Gardner 6HLW engines, and although ECW had redesigned the front and rear of the bus body

Of the 16 Bristol K5Gs purchased second-hand in the years 1955-7 the most handsome were arguably the lowbridge ECW-bodied pair acquired from Hants & Dorset. Resplendent in its new coat of paint at Newport is 789 (APR 426); note the rubber-mounted windows, indicating a degree of rebuilding by Hants & Dorset. *D. Clark*

One can almost hear the six-cylinder Gardner working hard in this view of Southern Vectis Bristol LD6G/ECW 556 (PDL 516) climbing St John's Road over the railway bridge in Ryde. One of the penultimate batch of LD models delivered in 1958, it would give 20 years' service, a fitting tribute to both chassis and body. *Alan B. Cross*

An idyllic scene featuring 1959 Bristol LD6G 556 (PDL 516) crossing the old bridge at Yarmouth. The bus has a huge dent in the front dome, which when sustained must have had the upper-deck passengers ducking in panic! *Michael Dryhurst*

Bristol's replacement for the semi-integral LS was the MW, with separate chassis and body. The coach version was nevertheless very similar to its predecessor, although the front and rear were more upright, in contrast to the more graceful curves of the LS, as apparent from this view of Southern Vectis 315 (PDL 515). Dating from 1958, this vehicle would be withdrawn from service in 1974 and happily is now preserved in the care of the Isle of Wight Bus & Coach Museum. *Glyn Kraemer-Johnson collection*

the coach version was little changed from that of the LS. The most noticeable difference was the fitting of a grille on the front panel, a requirement brought about by the fact that the MW had a front-mounted radiator, that on the LS being mounted behind the front axle; they also had two destination screens below the windscreens, replacing the winged motif of the LS, and a single, curved glass was fitted in the front dome.

The Lodekka too was undergoing further development. One of its drawbacks, albeit fairly minor, was the sunken gangway in the lower saloon. Working together, Bristol and ECW modified the design, reducing the size of the chassis side members, strength being gained from the rigidity of the body. At the same time the structure around the rear wheels was modified, making it possible to eliminate the raised seats forward of the wheel arch as well as the sunken gangway that had been features of the Lodekka since its inception. Thus, apart from the usual

pedestal below the longitudinal rear seats, the Lodekka had a completely flat and step-free floor throughout the lower deck — something our modern low-floor buses seem unable to achieve. The modified Lodekka was designated 'FS' in Bristol's logical fashion, the letters standing for 'Flat floor Short'. The Lodekkas delivered to Southern Vectis in 1960 were of this type, the now standard Gardner 6LW making them FS6Gs. Numbered 565/6 (TDL 998/9), they could be identified externally by the lower edge of the driver's cab window, which was straight rather than arching over the mudguard.

In July 1956 the maximum permitted length for double-deckers had been increased to 30ft, and, certainly by 1959, outside the Tilling Group, double-deckers of this size, usually with front or forward entrances, were becoming the norm. Leyland had designed its rear-engined Atlantean, offering seating capacities of up to 78, and by the end of the decade many operators were taking delivery of the type. Others were purchasing lightweight vehicles, often devoid of all but the basic necessities, in an effort to save fuel. Whilst some 30ft Lodekkas had been built, largely to rear-entrance layout, the Tilling Group seemed cocooned from these developments and continued in the main to take delivery of its 27ft rear-entrance 'deckers, seemingly oblivious to what was happening elsewhere. Within the next few years, however, all was set to change.

◄ The 1960 double-deck deliveries to the Southern Vectis fleet introduced Bristol's flat-floor FS-type Lodekka. This was distinguishable from the earlier LD type by the straight lower edge to the driver's cab windows, as illustrated by 566 (TDL 999) at Ryde Esplanade when new. *Photobus*

◄ A further pair of Bristol FS6G Lodekkas arrived in 1961, including 568 (VDL 845), seen climbing past thatched properties in Shanklin's picturesque Old Village *en route* to Niton. *Alan B. Cross*

6. WHERE'S YOUR ENGINE, MISTER?

In 1961/2 the last three Bristol L5Gs delivered to Southern Vectis (in 1946) were rebodied by Eastern Coach Works, prolonging the lives of otherwise serviceable chassis. They were given a full front and adapted for one-man operation, as apparent from the drop-down 'Pay As You Enter' sign on the front of 831 (EDL 16) at Albert Street, Ventnor. The engine was still located beside the driver, necessitating sound-deadening materials for not only the driver but the passengers as well. Note the fashions of the day, in particular the very narrow tie worn by the besuited young man strutting purposefully, possibly having just had his mohican hair styled and hoping not to be noticed!
Glyn Kraemer-Johnson collection

By 1961 the halcyon days of the bus industry were over. Glorious summer had turned to autumn, and a bleak winter was in prospect. Car ownership was on the increase, foreign holidays were becoming more popular, and the spread of television was keeping people at home in the evenings. All of these had their effect on bus operators, which, faced with ever-falling receipts, began to look for ways of cutting costs and increasing revenue. This could be achieved by cutting services, increasing fares or reducing manpower, and, whilst all were used, the latter was probably the one that had the most far-reaching effects.

Pay-as-you-enter buses had been used by Southern Vectis for years, and in 1958/9 they were seen as a way of avoiding the abandonment of several unremunerative services, including the Luccombe and Havenstreet routes. One-man operation (OMO) was seen as the way ahead, not only on the island but nationally. SVOC, however, had its hands tied to a certain extent. Apart from the Bedford OBs and the solitary Bristol LS its single-deckers were of rear-entrance, front-engine layout and were not suitable for this type of operation.

To help resolve the situation two 1946 Bristol L5Gs, 829/30, were sent to ECW for rebodying, 831 following a year later. ECW had developed a full-fronted forward-entrance body for the recently introduced Bristol SC chassis, and this formed the basis of the body used to give a new lease of life to both bus and coach versions of the Bristol L. In many cases the chassis were lengthened to give increased seating capacity, but this was not so with the SVOC examples, which retained their 35 seats.

Although unmistakably ECW the bodies did not have the elegance of the original half-cab design. The full front incorporated a bulge below the windscreen necessitated by the radiator, which was hidden behind an uninspiring if decorative grille. They had a narrow entrance with folding jack-knife doors positioned immediately behind the front wheels, and to enable the driver to collect the fares the front bulkhead was left unglazed, resulting in a noisy interior. Nevertheless they fulfilled a purpose and would remain in service until 1968/9.

More Duple-bodied Bedford SB8s entered service during 1961/2 together with two further batches of FS-type Lodekkas, these being the first 'deckers to be fitted with platform doors. The final batch, 569-73 (YDL 314-8), featured a revised style of radiator grille by then standard on all new Lodekkas.

By this time many of the Bedford OBs were nearing the end of their working lives, and a comparable replacement was required. Bristol had introduced its SC (**S**mall **C**apacity) chassis in 1954, but, although designed with one-man operation in mind, this was of front-engined layout, with the entrance behind the front wheels, and thus required the driver to turn through almost 180° to face his passengers. Operators were looking for a small underfloor-engined vehicle with a seating capacity of around 30, and in 1955 Albion had introduced just such a chassis, the Nimbus.

In 1956 Bristol introduced its SU (**S**mall **U**nderfloor), utilising the same four-cylinder Albion engine and other mechanical units used in the Nimbus. Two lengths were available, classified SUS and SUL, offering seating capacities of 30 and 36 respectively. Both models were 7ft 6in wide. ECW produced both bus and coach bodies to suit the new chassis. The coach version was almost a miniature version of the MW, with a small radiator reminiscent of that used on the Lodekka. The bus version was less attractive, with a shallow windscreen, of the same depth as the side windows, and a bulbous front incorporating a rectangular mesh grille devoid of trim. Being of a useful size and capacity, the bus version appealed to Southern Vectis, which took eight SUL4As. Delivered in the summer of 1963, 845-52 (458-65 ADL) were the company's first (and, as it would turn out, only) vehicles to be given reversed registrations.

Southern Vectis' final rear-entrance double-deckers arrived in 1962 in the shape of five FS6G Lodekkas featuring a new design of radiator grille. Not long after delivery, 570 (YDL 315) passes ex-Brighton, Hove & District Bristol K5G 902 (CAP 187) in Albert Street, Ventnor. *Alan B. Cross*

The Bristol SU was a lightweight type sharing many mechanical components with the Albion Nimbus, notably the four-cylinder engine. In 1963 Southern Vectis purchased eight ECW-bodied Bristol SUL4A models, of which 852 (465 ADL), numerically the last, is seen at Shanklin on local service 40 to the village of Luccombe. The photograph was taken in the early 1970s, when the Bristol RELL behind was virtually new. *Malcolm Keeping*

Following delivery of the last rear-entrance Bristol Lodekkas in 1962 the next new double-deckers to arrive on the Isle of Wight, in 1964, were of the longer, forward-entrance FLF type. Newport bus station is the venue for this nearside view of 601 (BDL 577B) on a glorious 27 August 1970. Because of the famous pop festival every serviceable bus was mustered for duty, hence the presence of ageing Bristol K types as well as recently delivered REs. *Alan Snatt*

By this time the general trend was for 30ft double-deckers to have the door positioned at the front in order that the driver could supervise loading and unloading, leaving the conductor free to collect the (hopefully) greater number of fares on a vehicle of increased capacity. A prototype 30ft forward-entrance Lodekka was delivered to the Bristol Omnibus Co in 1959, and full production began in the summer of 1960. The type was designated FLF (**F**lat Floor, **L**ong, **F**ront entrance). Whilst basically the same as the rear-entrance Lodekka the FLF had a more upright frontal profile, necessary to give sufficient room to upper-deck passengers ahead of the (forward) staircase. The layout here was more cumbersome than that on full-height buses, there being no seats beside the stairwell, simply a narrow gangway leading to the front seat, while the gearbox, which on the rear-entrance Lodekka had been concealed beneath a rearward-facing front seat, now intruded slightly into the lower saloon. The use of standard-size side windows meant that a small rearmost window was fitted on both decks. Once again Bristol and ECW had produced a simple and businesslike design, which proved to have the usual rugged reliability associated with their products and was arguably the finest model of the Lodekka range. The first examples for Southern Vectis were eight FLF6Gs with 70-seat bodywork, delivered in the autumn of 1964 as 600-7 (BDL 576-83B), thereby initiating another new numbering series. Further examples arrived over the next few years until a fleet of 22 had been amassed.

There were also developments on the coach front. Duple had redesigned its body for the Bedford SB, naming it the Bella Vega. Totally different from what had gone before, this had a wide, car-like grille, an almost straight waistline and a rearward-sloping pillar just ahead of the rear wheel, which gave the impression that the rear end had been stuck on as an afterthought. SVOC bought five, numbered 251-5 (ADL 104-8B). But stranger was to come, for consecutive registration numbers ADL 109/10B were applied to 401/2, again Bedfords but of the revolutionary VAL design. Powered by a Leyland O.400 diesel engine, this was a six-

wheel twin-steer chassis featuring the same size wheels as fitted to the diminutive 29-seat VAS. In contrast the VALs for Southern Vectis seated 52 and were the company's first 36ft vehicles, the maximum length for single-deckers having been increased in 1961. The chosen body, Duple's Vega Major, was very much a lengthened version of the Bella Vega fitted to the SBs.

The Bedford VAL achieved reasonable success throughout the country, but there always seemed to be more on the Isle of Wight than anywhere else. The model certainly found favour with Seaview Services, which over a period of time owned eight. All-Leyland PD2 GDL 765 was withdrawn in November 1963, and its successor, ADL 321B, delivered the following spring, was a Bedford VAL with a Willowbrook bus body built to a Duple design and seating 54 — one more than the double-decker it had replaced! Moreover it could be operated by one man, although the surviving lowbridge PD2 continued to operate alongside it.

Although the three 1946 L5Gs had been rebodied no new full-size single-deckers had been added to the fleet since the solitary LS saloon of 1953. By the early 1960s some of the LL5Gs had already been withdrawn, and the rest were nearing the end of their useful lives, if not due to their condition then by virtue of

their design and the need to have a conductor on board. Help was at hand, however, and in 1965 a trio of MW6Gs with 45-seat bodies were delivered. Nos 801-3 (EDL 234-6C) were handsome little buses and featured the winged motif in cream beneath the windscreen. A further four, 804-7 (FDL 925-8D), followed in 1966, together with three more Duple-bodied Bedford VALs for the coach fleet as 403-5 (EDL 992-4D).

The year 1966 was a sad one for the Isle of Wight, for despite much protestation it saw the closure of the Ryde–Cowes railway line and the Shanklin–Ventnor section of the Ryde–Ventnor line. The stretch between Ryde and Shanklin was reprieved on the understanding that it would be modernised. The truth of the matter was that to carry the hordes of passengers that disembarked from the ferries each Saturday in summer bound for Sandown and Shanklin would have taken a fleet of buses that would have completely clogged the surrounding roads. These closures had obvious effects on bus services. Additional journeys were operated on the 1/1A (Ryde–Newport–Cowes) and the 3 (Ryde–Newport via Havenstreet and Wootton), whilst a new service 39 was introduced to replace trains between Shanklin, Wroxall and Ventnor.

Despite a growing trend for foreign holidays as the 1960s progressed, the Isle of Wight continued to enjoy sunny days with a steady stream of visitors. They in turn needed moving on the 'Round the Island' trips, for which the twin-steer Bedford VAL was regarded by many operators as the ideal vehicle. How airy they were with the Duple Vega Major body with cant-level windows, as seen on Southern Vectis 402 (ADL 110B) at Ryde.
D. Clark

Often overlooked by enthusiasts was this 1964 Bedford VAL/Willowbrook operated by Seaview Services, the vehicle being overshadowed by the company's all-Leyland PD2s. In this view, recorded on 27 August 1970, ADL 321B stands by the railway line at Ryde Esplanade in the company of Southern Vectis Bristol LD6G 536 (LDL 735).
Alan Snatt

Between 1964 and 1971 Southern Vectis took 12 examples of the twin-steer Bedford VAL, including Duple-bodied 403 (EDL 992D), delivered in 1966 and seen here on excursion work. In traditional Southern Vectis livery it had an air of dignity that would be lost when repainted in all-over National white. *John Bishop / Online Transport Archive*

Although the ECW-bodied Bristol MW was apparently ideal for Southern Vectis, only nine were taken into stock, coaches 314/5 being delivered in 1958 and buses 801-7 in 1965/6. In full NBC livery, 804 (FDL 925D) basks in the spring sunshine while on layover at Alverstone in May 1976. The company's last MWs would be withdrawn the following year, but fortunately three — two buses and a coach — survive in preservation. *Phil Picken*

With the increased permitted length for single-deckers many
manufacturers, notably AEC and Leyland, had introduced
lengthened versions of their existing underfloor-engined chassis.
Bristol had chosen not to produce a 36ft MW, deciding that a
completely new chassis was required. The longer chassis, it was
envisaged, would be two to three tons heavier than the MW, and a
sturdier construction was needed. Moreover, having achieved a
step-free entrance on the Lodekka, Bristol was looking to do the
same on a single-decker rather than have the two deep steps
required on the underfloor-engined chassis. Leyland had achieved
an almost flat floor on its rear-engined Atlantean double-decker,
while Daimler had gone one better, providing a completely flat
floor on the comparable Fleetline, and both were enjoying good
sales. The increased length for single-deckers allowed for a
greater rear overhang and consequently more room for a rear
engine mounted horizontally beneath the floor rather than in a
separate pod at the back of the bus, as was the case with the
double-deckers. Hence the rear-engined chassis came into being,

christened (with characteristic simplicity) RE, for **R**ear **E**ngine.
What else? The chassis was offered, initially in long-wheelbase
form, with a choice of frame heights — low for bus work and
high for coach use, as the RELL and RELH respectively.

At this time the wind of change — or at least a gentle breeze —
was blowing through the industry. In 1962 the British Transport
Commission had been abolished and replaced by the Transport
Holding Company (THC), although there was no outward sign of
any change. The same year had seen a merger between Leyland
Motors and Associated Commercial Vehicles, the latter including
AEC and the bodybuilding concerns of Park Royal and Charles
H. Roe, the new enlarged organisation becoming the Leyland
Motor Corporation. Of more consequence to the THC was the
agreement reached in 1965 whereby Leyland acquired a 25%
holding in Bristol Commercial Vehicles and ECW, the THC
gaining a 30% share in Park Royal Vehicles. The outcome and
indeed the aim of this was that Bristol and ECW were now able
to sell their well-respected products on the open market.

At about the same time, Bristol updated its RE chassis, creating the Series 2 and also introduced a shorter 16ft 2in-wheelbase chassis, designated RESL or RESH according to frame height, capable of taking bodywork of between 30 and 33ft. Southern Vectis was the first Tilling Group company to take the RESL, four being delivered in February 1967. Numbered 808-11 (HDL 23-6E), they were of quite striking appearance. Most bus bodybuilders were producing what had become known as the standard BET single-decker, a functional 'no frills' design with peaked domes, a flat wrap-around rear window and a double-curvature windscreen. The initial ECW body for the RE bus was, in comparison, perhaps a little old-fashioned but none the worse

for that. It had a conventional rear dome with a central emergency exit flanked by two small windows. The front dome was similar to that on the MW, but the divided windscreen was of fixed glass, upright in profile but curving around the sides of the bus. Beneath this was a radiator grille of similar outline to that on the Lodekka, but much larger. Unlike some of its less successful competitors, the RE had a floor which was gently ramped towards the rear to clear the engine, offering a completely step-free interior.

Double-deckers delivered in 1967 comprised more FLF Lodekkas in the shape of 613-8 (GDL 768-71, 815/6E), while the coach fleet received Bedford VAL14s 406-9 (HDL 228-31E) with 52-seat Duple (Northern) bodywork.

In 1966 the THC had acquired no fewer than four of the island's coach operators — Fountain Coaches and Holmes Saloon Coaches, both of Cowes, and E. H. Crinage & Son and H. Randall & Sons, both of Ventnor. Rather strangely they were placed under the control of the long-established Bournemouth firm of Shamrock & Rambler (itself acquired by the THC in 1964). However, in 1969 the National Bus Company transferred Shamrock & Rambler's Isle of Wight operation to Southern Vectis control, along with a number of vehicles. This revived the Fountain Coaches fleetname, its vehicles being painted in Shamrock & Rambler orange and cream. In due course many of SVOC's own vehicles received this livery and fleetname.

By this time the original Bristol LS coaches, 303-7, were past their prime for front-line coach work although still sound in body and chassis. They were therefore sent to Strachans of Hamble for conversion to one-man buses. The conversion included the fitting of power-operated jack-knife doors, necessitating the modification of the nearside windscreen pillar and a dome-mounted bus-type destination box. Luggage racks were fitted reducing their capacity to 37, and they were painted in standard bus livery of Tilling green with cream window surrounds. In this form they lasted with the company until 1970/1.

In 1968 came quite an influx of new vehicles, including the last Lodekkas, FLFs 619-21 (KDL 143-5F). Two more RESL6Gs arrived, 812/3 (LDL 933/4G) introducing a revised body design, ECW having bowed to fashion and introduced new front and rear ends with peaked domes. They also had twin flat windscreens, slightly V-shaped in plan view; these were further modified for the 1969 deliveries, 814/5 (NDL 766/7G), being made deeper by extending them upwards into line with the tops of the side windows.

Whilst Seaview Services had a Bedford VAL for stage-carriage operations Southern Vectis used the type for excursion work. Duple-bodied 408 (HDL 230E) looks attractive in Tilling green and cream at Ryde Esplanade on 27 August 1970. Both chassis- and body-builder are now consigned to history, General Motors closing its UK commercial-vehicle subsidiary in 1987 and Duple closing completely in 1991. *Alan Snatt*

▲ Among the vehicles received by Southern Vectis with Shamrock & Rambler's Isle of Wight operations was this Duple-bodied Ford Thames 570E, 105 (XYO 10). New as a demonstrator, it had been acquired in 1963 by Fountain Coaches, whose livery it retained, as apparent from this view at Ryde. *Alan Snatt*

▲ A vehicle with a particularly interesting history was Southern Vectis 110 (517 ABL), a Duple-bodied Bedford SB8 new in 1962 to Thames Valley. Seen on 7 July 1973 at the coach park at Ryde alongside another SB8, native 247 (VDL 855), it had passed in 1968 to Fountain Coaches, which fleet had been acquired by Shamrock & Rambler in 1967 and was placed under Southern Vectis control in 1969. The Fountain Coaches name and orange livery would be retained for many years, in apparent defiance of the NBC corporate image. *Alan Snatt*

The coach fleet received more Bedfords, 421-6 (KDL 162-4F, MDL 597-9G) being VAM70s with Duple Viceroy bodywork featuring sliding vents in the cantrail above the main side windows, which produced quite a distinctive appearance. A particularly interesting vehicle, delivered in February 1968, was 301 (KDL 885F), a Bristol RESH 39-seat coach. Instead of the usual ECW coachwork however, it carried a Duple (Northern) Commander body, obviously from the same family as the Viceroy but without the cantrail windows and of quite imposing appearance. Originally fitted with a Gardner 6HLW engine, it proved desperately underpowered and was re-engined with the more powerful 6HLX. Only a handful of REs received this style of body, which makes its continued survival (in the Isle of Wight Bus & Coach Museum) all the more welcome.

The remaining two vehicles of 1968 were to yet another new Bristol design, the LH (Lightweight, Horizontal engine). This was effectively a replacement for the SU, being a lightweight underfloor-engined single-decker available in three lengths — 26ft (LHS), 30ft (LH) and 36ft (LHL). A choice of engines was offered — the 5.8-litre Perkins H6.354 or the 6.54-litre Leyland O.400 engine as used latterly in the Leyland Tiger Cub. Southern Vectis was again a very early user, taking the 13th and 14th production chassis. Nos 825/6 (LDL 262/3F were of type LH6L with 43-seat ECW bodywork. The body design owed much to the RE in its 'peaked dome' version, having the same front and rear end and the same pattern of radiator grille. However, the emergency exit was on the offside, allowing, for a single-piece rear window, and the windscreen, whilst of a similar style to the flat-screen RE, was extremely shallow, giving the bus a somewhat 'squashed' appearance and resulting in complaints from drivers about poor visibility.

Undoubtedly the most far-reaching event of 1968 was BET's sale of its bus interests to the Government. Thus Tilling and BET companies were now in the same stable, laying the foundation for the National Bus Company, which came into being on 1 January 1969. With initially little outward evidence of the change of ownership, apart from a few posters on the sides of buses proclaiming that Southern Vectis was 'proud to be a part of the National Bus Company', this was probably far from the truth and no more than wishful thinking on the part of senior management.

For a while vehicles continued to be delivered in Tilling green and cream with traditional gold underlined fleetnames. Another batch of Bristol LH single-deckers arrived in 1969 but were of the shorter LHS6L type and had 35-seat bodywork by a builder new to Southern Vectis, Marshall of Cambridge. Marshall had been building large numbers of single-deckers to the standard BET specification, but 832-5 (NDL 768-71G) were quite different. Whilst the basic outline was not dissimilar to the BET design, with peaked domes, the front featured a V-shaped windscreen, with separate angled corner windows, the whole having an aluminium surround. With the front panel devoid of any trim this tended to give them the appearance of a goods vehicle rather than a bus.

Mention the Bristol RE chassis and most enthusiasts will immediately picture the bus version, forgetting that a number were built as coaches; of these a few received Duple bodywork, including Southern Vectis 301 (KDL 885F), dating from 1968. *Alan Snatt*

By the late 1990s, when this view was recorded at Shanklin, 301 was on loan to the Isle of Wight Bus & Coach Museum, which in 2001 would finally acquire the vehicle — a worthy addition to its collection. *Dave Brown*

Introduced in the late 1960s, the Bristol LH fulfilled a need among many operators for a vehicle suited to lightly trafficked routes. With the relaxation of the requirement that Bristol and ECW products could be supplied only to state-owned companies came also a relaxation as to which builders could body Bristol chassis; illustrating this point when new is Southern Vectis 833 (NDL 769G), a Bristol LHS with Marshall bodywork of a style seen previously on Bedford chassis. Subsequent LH types for Southern Vectis would be bodied by ECW. *Malcolm Keeping*

Functional rather than handsome, the Marshall-bodied Bristol LHS6Ls of 1969 were enhanced in appearance by cream window surrounds, as demonstrated by 834 (NDL 770G) at Newport bus station on 27 August 1970. *Alan Snatt*

71

In 1968 Bristol launched its rear-engined VRT chassis, which, with the handsome Eastern Coach Works body, became the standard NBC double-decker. Representing the type is this early flat-screen example of Southern Vectis, 622 (NDL 490G), in Newport in October 1969. Note that at this time black lining was still being applied, while a weekly Rover ticket cost 39/6 (£1.97½); a daily ticket was 11/6 (57½p). *Glyn Kraemer-Johnson collection*

A fine view, recorded at Shanklin in July 1971, of recently delivered Bristol VR 625 (SDL 635J) in Tilling green. The flat windscreen of the early VRs gave the type a squarer and, in the opinion of this writer, better-proportioned look than did the curved BET screen fitted to later examples. *Dave Brown*

The final design of ECW bus body for the Bristol RE had a two-piece double-curvature windscreen and was introduced early in 1970; thus in a relatively short time the type had four versions of windscreen. Seen in Newport bus station on 27 August 1970 when only a few months old is 861 (PDL 492H) alongside an early Bristol Lodekka, LD6G 525 (LDL 724) of 1955. *Alan Snatt*

The new vehicles to cause most interest in 1969 were a pair of double-deckers, delivered in May. As mentioned in the previous chapter, the first Leyland Atlantean rear-engined double-deckers had entered service on the British mainland in 1958, being shortly followed by the Daimler Fleetline, and by 1969 production of the front-engined double-decker had all but ceased. Bristol had been a little slow off the mark, and it was not until 1966 that two prototype rear-engined double-deck chassis were built. They differed from the Atlantean and Fleetline in that, instead of being fitted across the rear, the engine was mounted at the rear offside, in line with the chassis. Had the design been perpetuated it would have had the benefit of being offered with a rear entrance/exit as well as or instead of ahead of the front wheels if so desired. With traditional Bristol logic the chassis was designated 'VRL' (**V**ertical **R**ear **L**ongitudinal engine) and was available in two lengths, 33ft and 36ft. A number of the longer VRLs were built, notably for Johannesburg and for Ribble subsidiary W. C. Standerwick, the latter having them fitted with stylish ECW double-deck coach bodies for its Lancashire–London express services. The longer chassis with extended rear overhang was necessary to accommodate the longitudinal engine, and when it was realised that most British operators preferred a double-decker of 30ft in length Bristol had to think again. There was insufficient room in a 30ft chassis to fit the engine in line, and so a new variant, the VRT, was introduced with rear engine mounted transversely, similar to the Atlantean and Fleetline. However, the engine was totally enclosed in the ECW bodywork, unlike the others whose engines were enclosed in a separate 'bustle' at the rear.

In July 1968 the Labour Government introduced the New Bus Grant, whereby operators could reclaim 25% of the cost of new vehicles provided they met the required specification, the idea being to encourage fleet replacement and increase one-man operation. The only double-deck design included was of 9.5m or 10m length with transverse rear engine, and this effectively sounded the death-knell for the original VR.

The first VRTs were delivered in late autumn 1968 to Scottish Omnibuses and were 33ft VRTLLs. The first VRTSLs, 30ft in length, were delivered to former Tilling Group companies between December 1968 and May 1969, Southern Vectis taking just two, as 622/3 (NDL 490/1G). The ECW body clearly showed signs of its ancestry, traces of the original postwar design being visible around the rear dome. The sides and upper-deck front were virtually the same as on the FLF, even to the small 'quarter' rear side windows. Jack-knife doors were sited forward of the front wheels. The windscreens were of the flat, slightly angled pattern used on the RE, and the front panel featured a horizontal moulding, rising over the headlamps, between which was a simple grille incorporating both Bristol and ECW badges.

More LHs arrived in 1970, with ECW bodywork but incorporating deeper windscreens and numbered 827-9 (PDL 489-91H). However, the two REs delivered that year, 861/2 (PDL 492/3H), which differed from previous examples in being of the 36ft RELL type, seating 49, were fitted with the BET-style double-curvature windscreen, producing, it must be admitted, a more modern-looking vehicle. The 1971 and 1972 deliveries followed a similar pattern, featuring further RELLs,

A unique vehicle in the Southern Vectis
fleet was 302 (XDL 122L), a Bristol
RELH6G with ECW's new style of
coach bodywork. Seen at Ryde in 1973,
it was to serve the company until 1988
and survives today in preservation.
Alan Snatt

The last coaches delivered in
traditional Southern Vectis livery of
Tilling green and cream were a pair of
Bedford YRTs with Duple Dominant
bodywork, which arrived early in
1973. Seen at Ryde when new, 413
(YDL 941L) would succumb to
National white in 1975. Two similar
coaches delivered in Fountain
Coaches' orange and cream would
retain those colours throughout the
1970s. *Alan Snatt*

VRTs, and Bedford VALs, the last two of which had Plaxton rather than Duple bodies. A new heavyweight coach was 302 (XDL 122L), a Bristol RELH6G with a new style of ECW coach body not dissimilar to the contemporary Plaxton product. This was among the last vehicles delivered in traditional Southern Vectis livery, the 1972 VRTs, 630-3 (XDL 377-80L),

with double-curvature BET-style windscreens, arriving in leaf green and white complete with the new NBC logo, a mirrored 'N' forming an arrowhead design. No 630 was exhibited at the 1972 Commercial Motor Show and also featured blue moquette upholstery with red and white 'double-N' symbols. The corporate image had arrived.

7. UNDER THE 'DOUBLE N'

By 1970, arguably, the 'glory days' of buses were over, not only on the Isle of Wight but everywhere. In fact in the eyes of many, your authors included, the bus industry reached an all-time low while under the control of the National Bus Company. Well-loved liveries disappeared, to be replaced by either leaf green or poppy red on buses, whilst coaches appeared in a bland allover white. Traditional and sometimes ornate fleetname styles gave way to plain block white letters applied in vinyl that had a habit of peeling off. The sides of coaches were emblazoned with huge red-and-blue '**NATIONAL**' fleetnames, applied with scant regard to vehicle design. Staff morale was at an all-time low, local control having been replaced by faceless management somewhere 'up there'. It was a time of shortages; shortages of drivers, shortages of spares and shortages of vehicles. For staff,

passengers and enthusiasts alike it was a depressing time and one which hardly fits the title of this book. It is therefore one that will be glossed over briefly.

Southern Vectis probably fared better than most under NBC control, its location safeguarding it from the mergers and changes of area that took place elsewhere. Moreover, whilst the livery of leaf green and white was hardly inspiring it was applied to the same layout as the Tilling green and cream it replaced, and it looked better on Bristol/ECW products than on many other types. Unlike those in a number of fleets, older Southern Vectis vehicles retained their black mudguards, which helped. In an effort to speed up the introduction of the 'corporate image' many buses had white waistbands applied to their Tilling green livery — and that *did* look awful!

One of a considerable number of Bedford VALs delivered to Southern Vectis in the years 1964-71, Duple Viceroy-bodied 408 (HDL 230E) had received National white livery by the time this photograph was taken in Newport. *Remember When*

The standard NBC double-decker was the Bristol VRT, which would doubtless have been SVOC's lot under the previous regime, although it was not without its problems, mechanical and otherwise. The VR was fractionally higher than the FLF and would not pass under the railway bridge at Moreton until the road was lowered. Scottish operators took a fervent dislike to the type, resulting in the great VR/FLF exchange of 1973 in which large numbers of Scottish VRs were transferred to NBC companies in exchange for Bristol FLFs. Southern Vectis gained three 77-seat Bristol VRTSLs, one from Central SMT and two from Eastern Scottish. They were downseated by SVOC to a more comfortable 74 and took the fleet numbers of the three F-registered FLFs they replaced, 619-21.

The first Southern Vectis coaches delivered in National white were three Duple Dominant-bodied Bedford YRTs new in the spring of 1974, among them 416 (ODL 866M), seen here on private-hire duty. *A. D. Packer*

Seen at Shanklin bus station *c*1975 are two early Southern Vectis Bristol RESLs, 1967 delivery 811 (HDL 26E) on the right and flat-screen 812 (LDL 933G) of 1968 on the left. The latter is in NBC leaf green, which in a black-and-white photograph looks little different from the traditional Tilling shade which 811 would retain until 1977. *Dave Packer*

By the mid-1970s the National Bus Company was very much in charge, witness the corporate fleetname and leaf-green livery adopted by Southern Vectis. Bristol LD6G 539 (LDL 729) nevertheless looked very smart when photographed in Shanklin in June 1976, having been given a fresh coat of paint, but rather surprisingly would soon be withdrawn. *Dave Brown*

With the downward sweep into the centre of the windows the rear of the Bristol Lodekka arguably had as much character as the front, as shown by this busy scene featuring LD6G 531 (LDL 730) at Shanklin bus station. Photographed in June 1976 in full NBC livery, the bus would be sold for scrap at the end of the season. *Dave Brown*

▼ Showing how the forward-entrance Lodekkas differed from their rear-entrance LD and FS cousins, 600 (BDL 576B), freshly attired in a coat of NBC leaf green, awaits passengers for Cowes in Ryde bus station in June 1976. *Dave Brown*

By the mid-1970s the scene at Ryde had changed; gone were the Tilling-green livery and underlined fleetname, in favour of the NBC corporate image. However, the Bristol/ECW fleet composition remained, Lodekkas being seen in the bus bays along with a lone RE. Behind is the footbridge over the railway line, whence many a photograph has been taken of the buses and trains, but taking pride of place in this view is Plaxton Panorama Elite-bodied Bedford YRT YDL 935L of Seaview Services. Note the simple telephone number (Seaview 3100) on the rear, with none of the dialling codes! *Dave Brown*

Both new and second-hand Bedford coaches continued to arrive, and SVOC somehow managed to continue painting many in orange and cream, with distinctly non-corporate 'FOUNTAIN COACHES' fleetnames.

If the Bristol VRT continued existing Southern Vectis vehicle policy, the standard NBC single-decker, the Leyland National, did not. Although the type proved exceptionally long-lived on the mainland it found little favour on the Isle of Wight, and SVOC's examples were disposed of with almost indecent haste, most being sold to other NBC or ex-NBC companies. None survived long enough to receive privatisation livery.

'The Old Girl', 1939 K5G CDL 899, survived the NBC period in Tilling cream and green, only a small 'double-N' radiator badge proclaiming its ownership. Sister DDL 50, however, suffered the indignity of receiving not only NBC green and white but also yellow and black stripes on her rear end when she was demoted to tree-lopping duties.

Seaview Services too had experienced changes. The remaining PD2, GDL 764, had been withdrawn in 1971, replaced by VDL 264K, a Bedford YRQ with Plaxton Derwent bus body. Thus the double-decker — and the conductor — were eliminated from the fleet. In 1979 the owner of Seaview Services retired and the company was bought by A. & M Robinson, who had been operating a two-coach firm in the Ryde area. There was little outward sign of its new ownership, the livery of two-tone green and red being retained.

By the end of the decade the VR was in need of updating. Leyland had designed its integral B15 Titan, but this had suffered all kinds of production problems and, with London Transport as its only committed customer, never really took off. In any case there was a need for a more flexible vehicle that could be offered in varying lengths for home and export markets. NBC companies wanted a bus comparable to the Bristol VR that could be built to an overall height of 13ft 8in and also expressed a preference for a vehicle with a separate chassis. Thus was born the Olympian, the first production model being delivered to Ribble in April 1981. Again Southern Vectis was an early user of the type, an initial six, with low-height ECW bodywork that bore a resemblance to the Titan, being taken into stock in April 1982. The Olympian, in its various forms, was to be the company's standard double-decker for the next 16 years.

Towards the end of its reign NBC ordered vast numbers of Mercedes L608Ds and Ford Transits whose van bodies were converted to minibuses by Alexander, Carlyle and PMT. Southern Vectis was the recipient of 21 Transits with Carlyle conversions. They were given red, blue or beige liveries and brand names according to the areas in which they operated, their size allowing them to penetrate hitherto unserved areas. The minibus lasted longer on the Isle of Wight than in many places, another 19 being purchased following privatisation, this time Ivecos with various makes of body.

The Transport Act of 1985 aimed to promote competition by the deregulation of bus services, which had existed since the 1930 Act. It also called for the dissolution of the National Bus Company and the sale of its various subsidiaries to the private sector. As so often happened, Southern Vectis was at the head of the queue, and on 8 October 1986 it was sold to its management, becoming the third NBC company to be privatised.

Foisted on the company by NBC, the Leyland National, in both short (10.3m) and long (11.3m) forms, made its debut in the Southern Vectis fleet in 1973. The earlier examples arrived in unrelieved green, but later deliveries had a white band and the corporate 'double-N' in red and blue on a white background. An 11.3m bus delivered in 1976 (unusually with the earlier style of roof pod), 880 (MDL 880R) is seen when almost new in Newport bus station, since consigned to history. The company's association with the National would be brief, and upon privatisation the last of the type would be banished from the island's shores. *Malcolm Keeping*

Replacement for the Bristol VR as NBC's standard double-decker was the Leyland Olympian. Delivered in 1982 and seen at Alum Bay when still relatively new, ECW-bodied 686 (RDL 686X) was the first example for Southern Vectis; along with the rest of its batch of six, it would remain in service on the Isle of Wight until 2003. *Glyn Kraemer-Johnson collection*

One can almost hear the scream of engine and gearbox as AEC Regent 901 (GW 6276) climbs the hill from Shanklin Esplanade into the town in June 1961. Note how the beading is picked out in the livery application. The fashions of the day also warrant attention, with long flowing dresses and the gentleman with the binoculars, seemingly oblivious to the sound emanating from 901. Acquired by Southern Vectis from Brighton, Hove & District in 1955 with others of the same type, this bus would be withdrawn later in 1961.
Dave Packer

One of a pair acquired from Brighton, Hove & District in 1955 to inaugurate open-top services on the Isle of Wight, Southern Vectis AEC Regent 900 (GP 6244), in cream livery with green relief, works Shanklin local service 45. New to Thomas Tilling in 1931 and rebodied by BH&D in 1945/6, it would see service on the island until 1960.
Alan Cross

For a premier holiday resort the Isle of Wight was surprisingly slow to adopt the open-top bus as a tourist attraction.

Brighton, Hove & District had inaugurated its famous Sea Front Service in 1936 using Tilling ST-type AEC Regents with new open-top bodies built by BH&D itself. It was not until 1957 that Southern Vectis introduced its first open-top service between Shanklin and Sandown, initially with two of those same Tilling AECs. Four of these veterans dating from 1931/2 had been bought, but in the event only two, 900/1 (GP 6244, GW 6276), were used. Both had been fitted with Gardner 5LW engines by BH&D. They were painted cream with Tilling green mudguards, bonnet and lining-out.

The service proved a success, and in 1959/60 Southern Vectis carried out its own conversion of the two K5Gs dating from 1939/40, 702/3 (CDL 899, DDL 50), little knowing at the time that by so doing they were saving these two magnificent vehicles for posterity. Unlike the BH&D vehicles, which had curved waistrails at the front and rear of the upper deck, the SVOC conversions featured a small two-piece windscreen at the front.

A new open-top service was introduced between Sandown Zoo and Ventnor, skirting the foot of St Boniface Down and offering spectacular views across Sandown Bay. A further service was started between Yarmouth and Alum Bay.

Two more second-hand open-toppers came from BH&D in 1960, 902/3

The road sign on the left indicates the hilly nature of the road from Shanklin to Ventnor. Bristol K5G/ECW 702 (CDL 899) reaches the summit near Luccombe, hotly pursued on its way to Ventnor by a classic Hillman Minx. Pictured in the 1970s, 702 is retained by Southern Vectis as a heritage vehicle and can regularly be seen on the road. *Dave Brown*

A sublime scene featuring 703 (DDL 50) in the old village of Shanklin *c*1970. Dating from 1940, the bus is a Bristol K5G with Eastern Coach Works bodywork converted to open-top in 1959. After operating for 10 years in this form it served as a tree-lopper for a further decade before final withdrawal in 1979. Thankfully it has been lovingly restored to original condition and is regularly seen at bus rallies. *Dave Brown*

A scene to gladden the heart of many an enthusiast as 903 (CAP 234), a 1940 Bristol K5G with Eastern Coach Works body converted to open-top by BH&D, makes its way through Shanklin Old Village. Acquired by Southern Vectis in 1960, this bus would serve the company until 1968, a testimony to the quality of the vehicle. Both authors heartily recommend the Crab Inn (right), mentioned in the Domesday Book. *Howard Butler*

(CAP 187, 243) being 1940 Bristol K5Gs that had been completely rebuilt by BH&D as convertible open-toppers and fitted with low PV2 radiators. Southern Vectis sold their roofs to Thorness Bay Holiday Camp, where they were incorporated into holiday chalets, and at least one was still in existence as recently as April 2000. No 903 itself survives in preservation.

The two vintage AECs were withdrawn in 1960/1, their places being taken by 904/5 (GL 6611/2), two 1939 Bristol K5Gs with Bristol's own BBW bodywork which, if anything, looked more archaic than the buses they were replacing. They came from Bristol Tramways, which had converted them for use at Weston-super-Mare.

A true Tilling atmosphere is provided by a line of Southern Vectis buses standing below the façade of Ventnor Town Hall in the early 1960s. At the head of the queue ex-Brighton, Hove & District Bristol K5G 903 (CAP 234) will soon be leaving on the picturesque hilly trip to Shanklin and Sandown; note the unusual white-on-red destination display used for open-top services. Behind can be seen 846 (459 ADL), a Bristol SUL4A, and further back, two FS-type Lodekkas and a K5G. *Howard Butler*

One of two such buses acquired in 1961 from the Bristol Omnibus Co, 905 (GL 6612) swings into Shanklin bus station. A standard Bristol K5G with body by BBW, the bus retains a prewar appearance, with its high radiator, six-bay window layout and the graceful curvature of the bodywork. It would serve Southern Vectis for just two years before withdrawal in 1963. *Howard Butler*

Southern Vectis Bristol K5G/ECW 907 (GHT 124) at Ryde Pier in the mid-1960s. New in 1940 to Bristol Tramways, it had been rebuilt as a convertible open-topper by second owner Brighton, Hove & District and moved to the Isle of Wight in 1962, although the roof was never used by Southern Vectis. When this photograph was taken in the 1960s British Road Services still played a prominent part in the transport scene, as depicted by Austin lorry ULD 189 in red livery. The Austin Devon and Austin Somerset cars are a timely reminder that 100 years have passed since the first Austin emerged from Longbridge in 1906. *Howard Butler*

The next two open-toppers also originated with Bristol Tramways. Nos 906/7 (FHT 112, GHT 124) had been amongst a number of K5Gs sold to Brighton, Hove & District in 1955 for conversion to convertible open-top in the same manner as 902/3. Acquired in 1962, they were used only in open-top form by Southern Vectis.

The demand for open-toppers seemed insatiable, another four being purchased in 1964, this time from Hants & Dorset. No 908 (FLJ 538) was a 1940 Bristol K5G that had been rebodied with a KS-style convertible open-top body but the roof had been irreparably damaged in 1960. The other three, 909-11 (FRU 303/4, GLJ 969), also K5Gs but dating from 1944, had been rebodied/rebuilt to full-fronted open-toppers by Hants & Dorset using a mixture of parts from their original bodies.

These veteran K5Gs maintained the open-top services into the NBC era when, in 1973, five LD-type Lodekkas, 541-5 (MDL 951-5) were converted to open-top. As with the previous SVOC conversions they had small upper-deck windscreens. They were renumbered OT1-5 and painted in NBC leaf green below the lower-deck windows and white above — possibly the most attractive application of NBC livery. They were joined in 1976 by a Bristol FLF6G. No OT6 (BRX 142B) had been new to Thames Valley, passing to Alder Valley on its

In 1964 Southern Vectis acquired four Bristol K-type double-deckers from Hants & Dorset for open-top services. This photograph, featuring 908 (FLJ 538) of 1940, is undated, but the advertisement promoting a week's travel for £2.40 (*i.e.* decimal currency) suggests that it was taken near the end of the vehicle's 10-year stint on the Isle of Wight. Judging by the number of passengers downstairs it must also have been on one of our so-called 'cool' summer days! *Michael Dryhurst*

Shanklin bus station in July 1971 is the setting for this marvellous view of 909 (FRU 303), a Bristol K5G new to Hants & Dorset in 1944 with Strachans bodywork. In 1952 it received this open-top body built by its original owner, although the modern-looking full front cannot disguise the dated six-bay layout. Acquired by Southern Vectis in 1964, it would nevertheless put in another nine years' service on the Isle of Wight. *Howard Butler*

formation, and had suffered damage from a low bridge.
Southern Vectis bought it in damaged condition and rebuilt it in
the same style as the LDs. It was painted in a silver livery with
blue waistband to mark the Queen's Silver Jubilee in 1977 and
retained this livery for the following season but lost its
commemorative lettering in favour of advertising for a local
DIY company. It was sold at the end of the 1978 season, allegedly
because drivers disliked it, but, as it could hardly have been very
different from SVOC's own FLFs, it is difficult to see why.

The first purpose-built convertible open-toppers arrived in
1979, when six standard Bristol VRTs, 671-6 (UDL 671-6S)
were sent to Hants & Dorset in exchange for six similar VRs,
705-10 (UFX 855-60S), but which had convertible-open-top
bodies.

Apart from CDL 899 and DDL 50 the most famous and
certainly the most unusual Southern Vectis open-topper must
surely be the 'Shanklin's Pony'. A standard Bristol RELL6G new

in 1971, 864 (TDL 564K) was rebuilt in 1986 to operate the
Shanklin Esplanade service (44). It retained its rear end below
cantrail level and the roof as far back as the first bay, the rest
being cut down to waist level. It was painted in a special yellow
and blue livery with the 'Shanklin's Pony' name on each side.

Following privatisation the open-top fleet appeared in a variety
of liveries, including blue, white and green 'Viewfinder' livery
(inflicted even on CDL 899!), apple green and cream, purple and
lime green and currently orange.

There was a brief period of competition on the Yarmouth–
Alum Bay service when Wightline Coaches of Newport bought
three open-top Leyland PD3s from Brighton Buses (that
connection again!) and commenced running a service 99 in direct
competition with Southern Vectis. The buses were turned out in
cream with what was almost Tilling green on mudguards and
around the upper-deck windows, the front and rear windows
and part of the dome having been retained as well as the lower

In 1979 six Bristol VRTs with ECW bodywork were received by Southern Vectis from fellow NBC subsidiary Hants & Dorset in exchange for a similar number of fixed-roof examples. In the style of leaf green and white originally applied to these buses on the Isle of Wight, 708 (UFX 858S) climbs away from Shanklin Esplanade, with Sandown Bay in the background. *Travel Lens*

Another of the convertible Bristol VRTs received from Hants & Dorset, 707 (UFX 857S), threads its way between the thatched cottages in Shanklin Old Village on its way to Luccombe, Upper Bonchurch and Ventnor in the summer of 1979. Regrettably this route, hugging the foot of St Boniface Down and offering spectacular views across Sandown Bay towards Culver Cliff, is no longer served by open-toppers. *Dave Brown*

A vehicle destined to remain unique on the Isle of Wight was 'Shanklin's Pony', photographed in its home town in June 1987. A standard Bristol RELL/ECW delivered in 1971, Southern Vectis 864 (TDL 564K) was converted to open-top in 1986, thereafter serving the company for another 14 years before passing into preservation. The 44 route linked Shanklin Esplanade with the town itself, tackling a spectacular climb in the process. *Glyn Kraemer-Johnson collection*

A popular location for enthusiasts when photographing open-top buses is Alum Bay, where the rolling downs descend abruptly to the sea. This late-1980s scene features Bristol LD6G 501 (MDL 952) of 1956 vintage in dedicated livery for the Alum Bay–Needles Battery service. Originally numbered 542, this bus was converted to open-top in the early 1970s and in this form would carry many a holidaymaker before finally being withdrawn from service in 2002. *Dave Brown*

part of the side windows. Red lettering promoted the service on the 'tween-decks panels.

In 1987 Southern Vectis had reached agreement with the National Trust whereby it could operate along the private road to the Needles Battery, another journey affording magnificent views of the coloured cliffs and across the Solent to the mainland. Wightline did not accept SVOC Rover tickets, as purchased by the majority of visitors, and the two factors together no doubt contributed to the demise of the operation. It ran for only one season, the buses being sold to London Sightseeing Tours.

Another novel open-top service was the 'Ventnor Buggy' operated by M Travel of Newport, a minibus operator that ran services in the Newport and Ventnor areas. The vehicle used was an ex-Southern Vectis Ford Transit cut down to open-top aft of the cab. A taped commentary was provided, and the bus had the advantage of being able to use some of the steep and tortuous roads at the back of Ventnor, which certainly couldn't have been traversed by full-size vehicles. Again, the venture lasted for only one season.

The final open-top operation was introduced in 1992 by Westbrook Travel, of Seaview. Numbered 88, the service started from Ryde, passing through Havenstreet, Robin Hill and across Brading Down to Sandown before returning to Ryde. It was operated in conjunction with Southern Vectis, the first and last journeys forming part of SVOC's service 8A. Two second-hand VRs were used, painted in a yellow and grey livery. The service now forms part of the Southern Vectis network.

For a while the service between The Needles and Yarmouth was worked by three of the MDL-registered Lodekkas (two having been reacquired from preservationists), but these were sold in 2002 for further use on Exmoor. In recent years a number of VRs and a couple of Olympians have been converted to open-top, retaining the forward portions of their roofs. The services are no longer numbered, being known as The Needles Tour, The Sandown Bay Tour and The Downs Tour.

One of the aims of the deregulation of bus services in 1986 was to promote competition and improve the quality of services. The Isle of Wight was no exception, and in 1993 Wightline came on the scene with its open-top service 99 between Yarmouth and Alum Bay, at the western extremity of the island, close to the famous Needles. Alas the service operated for but one season. Seen at Alum Bay, MCD 134F, was an MCW-bodied Leyland PD3 new to Brighton Corporation. *Dave Brown*

By the late 1980s the minibus was a feature of many a fleet, and Southern Vectis was no exception, running a fleet of Ivecos and Ford Transits. These could use roads impassable to conventional buses, as demonstrated by Ford Transit 259 (B259 MDL) close to the Buddle Inn, near Niton. Delivered in 1985, this vehicle would see six years' service on the island. *Dave Brown*

Following deregulation Southern Vectis experienced some competition from local operators, including Seaview Services, but after the initial skirmishes things settled down much as before.

Unable to expand within its own territory, Southern Vectis looked to the mainland and established Solent Blue Line operating in the Southampton and Eastleigh areas, today a flourishing company in its own right. Not so successful was an attack on Wilts & Dorset in Bournemouth and Poole, mounted jointly with Badgerline under the name of 'Badger Vectis', which probably meant nothing to anyone outside the industry. After a brief battle Badgerline and Southern Vectis retreated to their home territories.

The privatised Southern Vectis was launched with an attractive livery of emerald green with greensand (cream) window surrounds. This was replaced in 1995 by 'parchment' (a biscuity cream) with dark green skirt, roof and upper-deck window surrounds.

'Round the island' services 7/7A were introduced in 1993, branded as 'Island Explorer', and in 1998 eight new Volvo Olympians were delivered specifically for the service, painted in a two-tone blue livery with graphics and a huge 'Island Explorer' brand name; this was later simplified to allow commercial advertising to be applied. In 2000 the remaining double-deckers were painted in all-over red and branded as 'Route Rouge', a step that did not find favour with enthusiasts! Various single-deck

En route for Sandown via Shanklin, Leyland Olympian 714 (G714 WDL) of 1989 passes through the picturesque village of Godshill, with its thatched cottages. Seen in the attractive green and cream livery applied after deregulation and privatisation in 1986, this bus, along with others of its type, would subsequently (from 2001) wear the 'Route Rouge' livery, now discontinued following the Go-Ahead takeover in May 2005. *Dave Brown*

The first Olympians for Southern Vectis, with ECW bodywork, were delivered when the company was still under state control, the model having succeeded the Bristol VR as NBC's standard double-decker. Dating from 1984, 698 (A698 DDL) is seen at Godshill on route 2 to Cowes in the summer of 1997, wearing a different version of the 'deregulated' green and cream livery. *Dave Brown*

The mid-1990s saw Southern Vectis adopt an entirely new livery of green and mushroom, as portrayed by this view of 739 and 742 (K739/42 ODL) at the Buddle Inn, Niton, in the summer of 1995. Both vehicles are Leyland Olympians with Northern Counties bodywork delivered in 1993. Another development, in 1994, was the branding of the routes 7/7A as 'Island Explorer', as demonstrated by both vehicles. *Dave Brown*

The Bristol LHS was ideally
suited to the roads of the Isle
of Wight, and ECW-bodied
202 (KDL 202W) demonstrates
this admirably in Godshill
in the summer of 1998.
In all there were 16 of the
LH type delivered new to
Southern Vectis in the years
1969-81. No 202 was one of
the last batch of three LHS6Ls
new in 1981 and would remain
in service for 20 faithful years,
not being withdrawn until
2001. *Dave Brown*

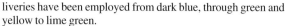

liveries have been employed from dark blue, through green and yellow to lime green.

The Olympian was the standard double-decker for the privatised company, with either Leyland or Northern Counties bodywork to a very high internal specification featuring tinted glass, high-backed coach-style seats and soft trim on sides and ceilings. Earlier ECW-bodied Olympians were upgraded to match. In 2002 the company's first low-floor double-deckers arrived in the shape of Volvo B7TLs with Plaxton President bodywork.

For a while there were no full-size single-deckers in the fleet, but gradually minibuses gave way to the ubiquitous Dennis Dart.

Possibly one of the best known features of Southern Vectis in the 1990s was a heritage fleet — a collection of Lodekkas, an MW and the sole remaining RELL, all wearing Tilling green and cream — which operated in service during the summer months. Alas this venture came to an end in 1997, allegedly because local residents objected to travelling on old buses, and the fleet passed to the Isle of Wight Bus & Coach Museum.

Whilst its near neighbours on the mainland passed into the hands of Stagecoach and FirstGroup, Southern Vectis survived to become one of the last ex-NBC companies to remain under its management's ownership. The bus industry appears to operate in 20-year cycles, and this certainly seems to be true of Southern Vectis. Formed in the 'Twenties, nationalised in the 'Forties, taken under NBC control in the 'Sixties and privatised in the 'Eighties, it finally sold out to one of the major groups in 2005. Fortunately the group concerned was Go-Ahead, which allows its subsidiaries to retain their individual identities and liveries. In the case of Southern Vectis one of its first actions was to create a new network of services and introduce a new livery. Out went the reds and blues to be replaced by a light and dark green so much more suited to the Garden Isle.

And, of course, the Go-Ahead Group also owns the Brighton & Hove Bus and Coach Co, the new name of the revived Brighton, Hove & District Omnibus Co. The Brighton connection is complete!

How many enthusiasts have one of these in their home? Still to be found near Newport as recently as 1998 was this old cast-iron Southern Vectis bus stop. At one time Tilling companies generally had very similar stops, but these have been banished in favour of the internationally recognised design with a picture of a bus —just in case its purpose is unclear . . .
Dave Brown

Following the takeover by Go-Ahead Group Southern Vectis reverted to a green livery. Bound for Ryde, Northern Counties-bodied Leyland Olympian 737 (K737 ODL), now named *Watershoot Bay*, is seen pulling away from the stop in Albert Street, Ventnor, in May 2006. *Glyn Kraemer-Johnson*

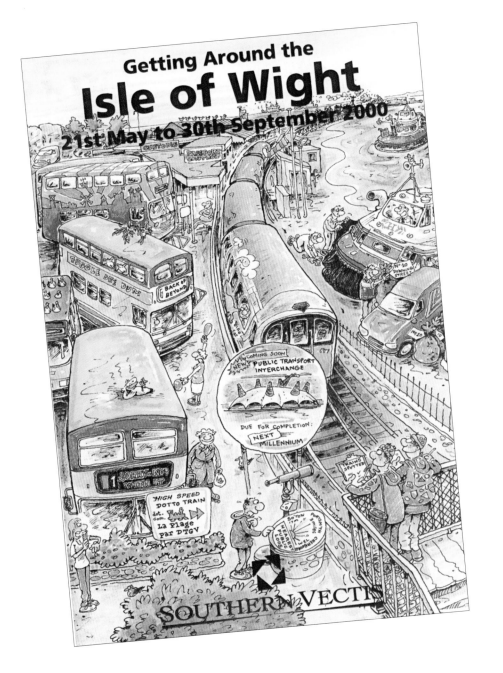

SOUTHERN V

Savoy (for Fort

Colwell Bay

Totland   FRES

Alum Bay   Fre

The Needles

7 7A
11 12
42

42

MAIN BUS SE
on the
ISLE OF WI
(also showing train stations &
LOCAL BUSES in Freshwat
Sandown and Shanklin are
on this map